T0294212

Kristy Chambers was born in Adelaide, South Australia, in 1975. After graduating from university as a nurse at age thirty, she worked in several hospitals before writing the bestselling memoir *Get Well Soon! My (Un)Brilliant Career as a Nurse* (UQP, 2012). She currently lives in New York City, where she writes books and scoffs bagels. Check out kristychambers.com.au for more.

KRISTY CHAMBERS

IT'S NOT YOU, GEOGRAPHY, IT'S ME

UQP

First published 2014 by University of Queensland Press
PO Box 6042, St Lucia, Queensland 4067 Australia

www.uqp.com.au
www.kristychambers.com.au

© 2014 Kristy Chambers

This book is copyright. Except for private study, research, criticism or reviews, as
permitted under the Copyright Act, no part of this book may be reproduced, stored
in a retrieval system, or transmitted in any form or by any means without prior
written permission. Enquiries should be made to the publisher.

Cataloguing-in-Publication entry is available from the
National Library of Australia
http://catalogue.nla.gov.au/

ISBN (pbk) 978 0 7022 5324 9
ISBN (ePdf) 978 0 7022 5302 7
ISBN (ePUB) 978 0 7022 5303 4
ISBN (kindle) 978 0 7022 5304 1

Author photograph by Stephen Booth
Typeset in 11.5/16pt Bembo by Post Pre-press Group, Brisbane
Printed in Australia by McPherson's Printing Group

University of Queensland Press uses papers that are natural, renewable and
recyclable products made from wood grown in sustainable forests. The logging and
manufacturing processes conform to the environmental regulations of the country
of origin.

For Ciara and Izzy

Contents

1   It's Not You, Geography, It's Me

Whenever I told people that my second book was going to be about 'mental illness and travel', the initial response was usually, 'Oh ... that sounds interesting', said in such a way that it seemed like the person thought *maybe* it would be interesting, but it certainly didn't sound very funny, and actually, it probably wouldn't really be that interesting either.

I can understand that. Reading about other people's travel experiences is only slightly less painful than being forced to sit through a slide show of someone else's holiday snaps, which is sort of like being told about a party you didn't go to.

The travel book is marginally superior to the photographic slide show, though, because at least you can put it down when you're bored without hurting anyone's feelings – the writer will never know that you couldn't give two shits about the time they went to Romania and milked a goat.

A book about mental illness, however, sounds about as appetising as a bowl of shoe polish and conjures images of dry textbooks or bleeding-heart self-help manuals of the *Oh My God, You're A Mess! Let Me Fix You!* variety. A book mixing travel *and* mental illness sounds like a soup made of yawns and tears. Delicious.

And what do these two topics have to do with each other anyway, I hear nobody ask, and the sound of crickets chirping. Well, for me, travel and mental illness go together like coffee and getting shit done. Also answering to the names of 'running away' and 'escapism', travel has been my drug of choice, along with prescribed medication, alcohol and movies, for the depression that has been a bug up my ass since I was fifteen. Travel has always given me much more than I expected, even if it was more diarrhoea, anxiety and boredom than I ever thought possible, but it took a while for me to understand that it could never be a cure-all for unhappiness.

For a really long time, I thought that happiness could be found somewhere other than where I was; that it was a place that existed outside my head, like Iceland or Tasmania, and if I just kept looking, I'd eventually stumble across my peace of mind in a faraway place. Of the many delusions that I have entertained in my life, such as the idea that there is a weight at which I will be satisfied or a gym membership that I'll use for more than two weeks, the belief that the grass is greener elsewhere has always been the most entrenched (although there is a town called Hell in Norway and I expect that the grass there is probably scorched, if not dead).

One notion I never bought, though, was that our high school years are the best of our lives. Whoever came up with that idea probably also believed that Christmas was the most wonderful time of the year. I beg to differ. I find my birthday, not Christmas, to be the most wonderful time of the year, the day itself and the days after it until all the cake is gone, and quite frankly, my high school years were some of the worst of my life.

Really, how could anyone love high school? Being a teenager is terrible. Imagine knowing everything about everything and having to sit in a classroom for six hours a day listening to some old fart when your primary focus is navigating the existing social hierarchy so that you're situated somewhere closer to the top than the bottom. Homework and parents just get in your way; 'puppy fat' becomes plain old 'fat' and all of this tumultuousness occurs under the monstrous umbrella of puberty, an ugly word for an even uglier time. I'm not sure which part of that I'm supposed to cherish. And to add insult to injury, I met my nemesis, depression, around the time of my fifteenth birthday.

In March 1990, every blood relation on my mother's side had travelled to Sydney for my grandmother Marie's eightieth birthday party, an informal backyard barbecue that also doubled as a family reunion, and the first inkling that something was wrong with me was that I had lost my appetite. I declined the offer of birthday cake, and that *never* happens. By the time we returned home I was unwell and spiking pizza-oven temperatures.

When my eyes and skin began to acquire a faint yellowish hue I was back at the doctor's office and what was initially suspected to be a severe bout of flu turned out to be glandular fever, accompanied by an inflamed liver. According to my blood tests I had the liver function of a fifty-year-old alcoholic, without ever having experienced the joy of a weekend bender or being found passed out in a pool of my own urine. I had skipped all that stuff and gone directly to hepatitis. After a few weeks spent resting in bed, I returned to school, still fatigued and feeling fragile but thankfully no longer the colour of butter.

Saying that you were unhappy as a teenager is like pointing out that water is wet, but when I went back to school I felt unhappiness of a new persuasion. Something was off with me, and although I couldn't articulate what it was, I began to feel overwhelmed by things that normally wouldn't bother me. When I failed a test and argued with a friend on the same afternoon a few days later, these laughably trivial upsets resonated like a natural disaster in my teenage world. I'm not generally a fan of conflict or failure, least of all those involving me, and while either would have been upsetting in ordinary circumstances, the pain I felt was never so white hot as this. I was all wound up with nowhere to go, like an animal with its leg stuck in a trap.

As my brother, sister and I all waited, as usual, in the shade of the huge peppercorn tree at the front of school for our ride home, out of nowhere my mind produced a shockingly simple remedy for my anguish: *You could just kill yourself, you know.*

4

Something clicked in my brain, like a cartoon light bulb switching on above my head, and I felt a flood of relief and euphoria. Suddenly there was a very obvious way out, and it was a way out of *everything*. I couldn't believe it had taken until now for me to think of it. When I got home, I took a glass of water from the bathroom, a box of pills from the medicine cabinet, then went to my room and swallowed them in handfuls. My happiness disintegrated as I wrote a letter saying sorry and goodbye to my family.

The sensation of freedom was short-lived. As I lay on my bed, crying and waiting for what came next with a stomach full of pills, I got scared. I didn't want to live, but I also didn't want to die; I was in a real pickle.

Soon I was in the emergency department, being stabbed with a cannula by an unskilled intern and throwing up into a hospital sick bowl as my mum rubbed my back. Thankfully, this was before Google, before the 'information superhighway' even existed, and I had just swallowed whatever was at hand and not painstakingly researched a medication that would result in maximum harm. The twenty-two clear capsules filled with tiny coloured balls I'd taken were antibiotics, and they might not have done anything more than give me diarrhoea and a nasty stomach-ache, but as they say, it's the thought that counts.

I was kept in hospital overnight for observation and in the morning a child and adolescent psychiatrist came to see me. He put a name to the way I felt and told me that I had clinical depression, I was sick. He said that glandular fever and depression often went hand in hand, but as there was a family history of depression on my dad's side, it may have been going to happen anyway; perhaps the glandular fever had just hastened its inevitable arrival. That there was an explanation for what I was experiencing was encouraging, even if I continued to feel like shit, because my 'cry for help' had bought me some space, some time out from life, but fundamentally nothing had changed. I felt hollow and worn out.

On the way home from the hospital, my mother said that it was one thing to think about suicide and another to take concrete steps towards it and that she was relieved that we didn't have a gun in our house. She couldn't bear to think that I might have done something I couldn't come back from and asked me to promise that I wouldn't do anything like that again. I agreed. (She did the same thing when I came home with a tattoo. Some might call it emotional blackmail, others exceptional parenting, but either way I'm still here, and with just a single tattoo to my name.)

Making that promise was easy at the time; I was numb and exhausted and functioning on automatic pilot, but once I'd crossed over to suicidal thought, there was no going back. I kept my promise not to *act* on the thoughts, but that didn't stop the thoughts from recurring. It was a sick sort of release, a coping technique that activated automatically when I hit a particularly miserable plateau. The suicidal light bulb that had switched on above my head was seemingly on for good.

There was a long recuperation period afterwards, with lots of sleep and daytime television, and I didn't tell anybody what had happened because I thought people wouldn't understand. This wasn't the sort of thing you talked about, so it became a family secret. Having an illness that could be easily understood, like glandular fever, was a good cover for another illness that could not.

The overdose was just the beginning, as it turned out, and not even close to the end, thwarted or otherwise. After a year and a half of relapsing sadness, my mother took me to see the doctor, again, seeking a solution for what was turning out to be a persistent, complicated problem. I was the first teenager my parents had raised, so there was nobody to compare me with, but my constant tearfulness, tiredness, and looking and feeling 'flat' clearly went beyond the expected moodiness of adolescence. I was almost seventeen, and the doctor said the only thing he could suggest was medication, but even he seemed uncertain about it. At that time Prozac was the 'next big thing', but there was still quite a stigma attached to antidepressants and that was nothing compared with the shameful stigma attached like a bloodthirsty leech to mental illness in general. I didn't like the idea of being on medication, and neither did my mother.

When the doctor said, 'Then I don't really know what I can do for you', I remember the resignation I felt. *Well, that's that.* It was almost a relief to find out that nobody was going to be able to fix me and to surrender any false hope. I *was* really on my own, it didn't just feel that way, so I decided I would deal with it by pulling my socks up and plastering a smile on my face and that in the future I would try harder to be happy. If the definition of insanity is doing the same thing over and over but expecting a different result, then I wasn't just depressed, I was insane.

The next five years were marked by a yawningly repetitive cycle: crash, rest, revive. The depression came and went, but it always returned every three to six months like a Jehovah's Witness knocking at the door. I tried every non-invasive treatment available because, above all, depression is *fucking boring*. It's about as exciting as watching paint dry, except the paint is invisible, hates itself and is coating a guilt and self-loathing machine. Intellectually, you know that the way you're feeling is baseless and that you *should* be happy, but you're not. People are dying from hunger, disease and war, and *you're* depressed?

You have quite a nerve!

My audacity didn't go unpunished. I beat myself up for it regularly. The inside of my head was not a nice place to be, and on the outside, I was lurching from one unfulfilling retail job to the next after dropping out of university twice in as many years. After managing six months of a Creative Arts degree before losing interest, I took a stab at a degree in education. It was a stint that lasted just two weeks, colliding with the arrival of another low ebb, and I abandoned the idea of studying altogether and focused on trying to feel better.

I saw a naturopath and tried cutting out dairy, sugar, meat and white flour, which was its own unique brand of misery. I slept twelve hours a night. I exercised every day. I had intravenous vitamins and acupuncture. I lived in different places. I took up smoking. I got drunk. I stayed up all night writing in my diary. I played guitar. A lot of things helped, but nothing provided sustained relief. I could function, for a while, and then I would fall in a heap again. I was basically a parachute.

Each bout of depression wore me out a little bit more than the last. Eventually I was so sick of it that I started to daydream wistfully about dying, in the way that I would previously have thought about travelling the world or getting a dog – nurtured dreams that weren't immediately possible. I wanted to disappear, to climb back into the womb, return to nothingness and never exist. As my desperation increased, my thought processes became more twisted and I asked my parents if they had wanted me, if I had been an accident. Maybe I was never supposed to be born and I had sensed it in utero and that was why I didn't want to live. It was clearly time for more drastic action. I was losing it.

A friend of a friend recommended a new doctor, and when I went to see her and told her how I had been feeling, the same old story I was tired of telling, she patted my hand kindly and said, 'You poor thing. Your brain just isn't making enough happy chemicals. We can fix that with some tablets. Don't worry.'

I wanted to believe her more than I actually did because it had been going on for so long (six years) that I thought it was hopeless and my cross to bear for life.

After seeing a psychiatrist who agreed that medication was necessary, I was started on a small dose of the antidepressant Zoloft, and initially I didn't *just* feel depressed, but also like I'd contracted some kind of nuclear flu. I sweated, clenched my jaw and ground my teeth. My pupils were huge, sleep was elusive and I had no appetite – I felt like a zombie and looked like a bag of crap.

After two weeks the cloud around me lifted briefly, giving me a glimpse of something brighter, but it quickly returned, and I was right back where I started, which was not a place I wanted to be anymore. I went back to the doctor and reported my progress, or lack thereof.

She increased my dose and I waited for something to happen, but nothing seemed to. I slept a lot and very gradually began to feel less fried and my saliva started to lose its metallic taste.

Six weeks later, the unpleasant side effects described on the medication leaflet had subsided, for the most part, and I emerged from my chemical cocoon like the clichéd butterfly. It was alien to me, but I felt happy, and it wasn't fleeting like the fast food 'happy' I found when I was drunk.

'So *this* is how people are meant to feel,' I thought. The sensation, overall, was like growing a missing layer of skin – the necessary buffer between the world and me. I felt I could cope with life, and it was the first time I could say so with any confidence.

The exuberance I initially felt, perhaps partly explained by the great contrast to feeling like shit for so long, eventually settled down to a more subdued backdrop of wellbeing. I wasn't cheerful all the time, but I knew I had the potential to be, and the lows were less frequent and much easier to overcome.

While I might sound like a cheerleader for Pfizer, being on medication isn't all beer and skittles. There was one side effect that stayed a lot longer than the others and of all the possible complications it had initially seemed the least troublesome on paper.

'Inability to experience orgasm, delayed orgasm, decreased libido ...' Since I wasn't exactly dating up a storm in my melancholia, the only activity occurring in my bedroom was an excessive amount of sleep so I was perfectly willing to throw my libido on the fire if it would make me feel better – that is, until I felt better, and then I resented it.

When you're sitting in the dark wishing that your life would just *end*, the idea of impaired sexual functioning is not such a big a deal in comparison, but it was still disappointing to discover that the emotional numbness the medication originally provided made *everything* kind of numb, and physical sensation was muted, like being underwater. Taking medication may have made me feel like I wasn't failing at life in its entirety anymore, but it certainly felt like I was failing at a particular part of it. *Wham, bam, thank you ma'am* was more like *Wham ... bam ... uh, hello? Is anybody home?*

I can only imagine how confronting it is for men. *Oh, you thought you were depressed before? Well, how do you like this, numb-nuts?*

You didn't have to be a sex fiend to feel hard done by in this situation, although that would definitely help. I found that the sensory bluntness medication imbues does eventually fade (perhaps, too, does its efficacy), but sexual dysfunction, or just less than stellar sexual function, can be a big obstacle to overcome. When you're feeling happier in every way but semi-comatose from the waist down, you start to notice the things that are missing, making it easier to forget what you've gained.

Perhaps if there were a quick and convenient way to measure neurotransmitter levels in the brain, like pricking your finger to test your blood glucose, people like me would take their medication and never waver. 'Your brain is deficient in a certain chemical,' the test would show, 'and for this you may take an oral supplement, much like a vitamin. Rest assured that this is not a sign of weakness or insanity. It's just sensible.'

The trick with antidepressants, though, is that if they work and you feel happy, you start to think that you don't need them anymore. After about six months I thought, 'I feel fine. Why am I taking a drug for depression when I'm not depressed anymore?' So I stopped, and in a few months I became depressed again and restarted my medication. This process was repeated a number of times in the first few years and I've come to realise that this dizzying roundabout is practically a rite of passage where depression is concerned, and that the vicious cycle repeats itself until one day you finally accept that you have an ILLNESS THAT IS CONTROLLED BY MEDICATION. So for the love of Christ, just *take them* and stop messing with yourself. Taking medication isn't the end of the world; it's what stops me feeling that the world ending wouldn't be such a bad thing.

When I originally began taking medication, I thought that it would be a short-term thing, maybe even a longish short-term thing, but that it would be finite and at some point I wouldn't need it anymore. Unless I have a brain transplant, I don't see that happening, and I'm okay with it. If your blood pressure is high and all else fails, you take a pill to bring it down. And when it does, you know the pills work and you continue taking them to stay well. You don't think, 'Hey, I'm better! I don't need these!' and throw them in the garbage. But there is no shame in taking medication to make your heart behave, and no precise measurement of despair.

2   Upper Slaughter

So, you've found an antidepressant that works for you? *Congratulations!*

What now?

My life had been a very stop-start affair before I began taking medication, similar in motion to me driving a car with a manual transmission, but now that my ship was relatively shipshape, I had to figure out what to do with it. Being a former professionally depressed person is fine, but it's not a 'career' as such, although I didn't think I would ever want one of those. A career sounded like something you pursued when all your childhood dreams were broken, and it also sounded like something that would require me to brush my hair. The only thing I knew beyond a shadow of a doubt was that I wanted to see what the rest of the world looked like.

Travel is an excellent way of *not* making a decision about your future while giving the general impression that you have. And working a dead-end, poorly paid job overseas is much better for your self-esteem than doing the same job at home, so I decided I was getting out of town. I worked in retail for eighteen months, saved as much money as I could and bought myself a backpack and a ticket to London. A number of my friends who had stuck out their university degrees and graduated were already living there and doing the same thing.

As an Australian citizen, I was eligible to apply for a Working Holiday visa that permitted me to live and work in the United Kingdom for two years and made exploring Europe a piece of gateau. Because living in Australia is sort of like living on the moon, flights from it to anywhere else are expensive, so being based in England was a much more economical way to maximise travel ... in theory.

As soon as my plane touched down at Heathrow two-thirds of my savings disappeared into the ether because the Australian dollar was worth a crushing thirty-three pence at the time, and the remaining third began to haemorrhage when I paid for things in pounds sterling but confused the price with Australian dollars. By nightfall of the first day I had accidentally bought myself a very expensive winter coat on Carnaby Street because I was so cold I rather dramatically thought I was going to die.

I had only been in London for a week and a half, seeing all the touristy stuff like Big Ben and Buckingham Palace, when an ATM account balance showed me the error of my ways. If I didn't leave soon I'd have to get that overseas dead-end job I was already not looking forward to, so I met up with two friends from Australia, Shaun and Rachael, and we all went to Paris together.

And then, *I was in Paris*, a city I'd always dreamt of visiting and there really was as much dog shit on the streets as I had heard and even the *supermarché* was exciting, with three aisles of assorted groceries and six for wine and cheese. We went to the Louvre, climbed the Eiffel Tower, ate French food, did terrible things to their beautiful language, got frowned at and constantly yelled at each other that we either could, or could not, believe we were in Paris.

'I CANNOT BELIEVE WE'RE IN PARIS!' someone would shout, followed by the counter response, 'WE ARE! WE'RE REALLY IN *PARIS*!'

I felt high on life for the first week in France, and then things began to sour. As a stubborn dreamer, I offer the worst of both worlds – I'm completely unrealistic about pretty much everything, and yet I also refuse to budge an inch. Having a vivid imagination is great, unless you take what it produces seriously and expect it to be replicated in real life. That's how you end up in jail for stalking Brad Pitt because you think he's your boyfriend and can't understand what you did to make him lock you out of the house when you thought things were going so *well* in your relationship.

Somewhere along the line, probably in the year of committed daydreaming I'd done prior to leaving, I had formulated the idea that packing all my clothes into a bag and carting it around Europe like a snail would equate to the kind of joy a dog feels when rolling in something stinky. Additionally, I expected that there would be some sort of travel-induced epiphany early on where my calling in life would become rapturously clear.

This was incorrect.

It didn't take long for me to realise that travelling to other countries does not automatically make you a happy person, or an interesting one, or even a reasonable human being if you weren't one to begin with. If you're a shitbag at home, you'll be a sac de merde in Paris. And even with the cushioning of Zoloft, the excitement of being somewhere new and the freedom to do what you want, the feeling that you're a lost soul is going to break the surface eventually.

If there's only one thing I learnt in high school physics (there is) it's that Sir Isaac Newton coined the phrase 'What goes up must come down!', which was like the 'YOLO' of his day. I don't give two hoots about gravity, or how it keeps me magically tethered to the earth's surface, but I have always found Newton's pronouncement comforting. If what goes up *must* come down, then what goes down must come up again, too. It's something I tell myself when I'm feeling bad, and it's what I told myself when I was feeling bad in Belgium.

Three weeks into my trip, I was sitting by an icy lake, eating a waffle and feeling undeniably flat. It wasn't the kind of unhappiness I felt before I started taking medication, but it was the worst I had been in quite a while, and feeling any kind of negative emotion while eating a freshly cooked hot sugar waffle is no mean feat. Shaun and Rachael were enjoying themselves just fine, but I was sinking.

Running away to Europe had been my dream for so long, but the way I felt living it, the picture I was standing in, bore little correlation to the dream. I had expected my life to play out like a movie. I had expected to be happy, and I wasn't.

The disparity between fantasy and reality was a significant, self-inflicted injury but I didn't know if it was solely responsible for my mood. Perhaps it was environmental, due to an unfamiliar lack of sunshine and freezing weather, or maybe it was because my lunch was a waffle. My greatest fear, though, was that it was because there was just no pleasing me, and even when I got what I wanted, or got what I *thought* I wanted, it was never going to be enough.

The thing I didn't understand then, and for many years after, was that taking medication for depression only meant my condition was no longer debilitating – the happiness part was always going to be up to me. I was taking Zoloft, not the magic beans from *Jack and the Beanstalk*, and there was only so much it could do. Expecting a tablet to provide endless happiness was like paying for a gym membership but never going to the gym and still expecting to get in shape. Happiness was something I'd have to work at, and keep working at, even if I didn't want to shoulder the responsibility and often let it drop to the floor like a carton of eggs, creating quite a mess.

The decline in mood that occurred in Belgium, despite the presence of some of the world's best chocolate, fries and waffles (and an amusing statue of a pissing boy), was confusing to say the least. It didn't lift in Amsterdam, where

I parted ways with Shaun and Rachael, opting to travel on to Germany alone instead of joining them in Switzerland. I was still feeling crappy by the time I got to Berlin, so I made a reverse-charge call to my mum and told her I didn't understand why I wasn't having the time of my life when, by all accounts, I should be. It felt good to admit it, although learning later that my hour-long phone call cost $300 didn't, and it wasn't long before I rebounded. And by 'rebounded' I mean I ricocheted from one end of the mood spectrum to the other like a rubber band flicked across a classroom by a naughty kid.

For me, the simplest kinds of magic come from believing in Santa and drinking alcohol. Santa is very calendar-specific, so if I'm looking for a temporary remedy, alcohol is always it. Combining alcohol, a depressant, with anti-depressants is not a good idea, much like eating a bucket of fried chicken while on a treadmill or using one of your body parts to check if a fire is hot (they're always hot). Alcohol impairs the medication's ability to work, but if you already feel that your medication isn't working, you can see the chain of thought that begins calling, and ordering, the shots.

When I got to Prague in the Czech Republic and discovered that the beer was cheaper than bottled water, I began drinking it like bottled water, while continuing to take my medication. And within a few days I found myself enjoying not only Eastern European prices and an abundance of Gothic architecture, but a brand new state of mind – mania.

'Enjoying' is an understatement. I barely slept or ate and had the kind of boundless energy I could sometimes find if I drank a bucket of coffee, which invariably ended with insomnia and a splitting headache. I had no idea what was occurring inside my skull, but the intense high I was experiencing was much more fun than the angst-ridden lows I was accustomed to. I sent my parents a jubilant email announcing that not only had my bad mood passed, but that I was having the best time ever and they didn't have to worry about me anymore because I was never going to be unhappy again. They sent one back that said, 'Are you on drugs?'

After all the down periods I'd experienced it seemed only fair to me, in a way, that I should bounce back with such an effervescent 'up'. The only danger was that because I felt like the king of the world, consequences were not a priority.

In Prague I became the sort of loathsome tourist I'd always looked down on, the kind that climbs up on a statue in the Old Town Square at two in the morning to enjoy a better view of the area while drinking a large glass of beer. Not everybody agreed with the impulsive voice in my head that told me it was a good idea. The policemen who suddenly appeared at the edge of the square and began walking towards me had very stern expressions and guns; they were *literally* the fun police. I waved hello.

'*Down!*' one of them commanded, motioning with his hand. I complied, clumsily, abandoning my glass on the ledge.

'Passport,' the other demanded, and even though my passport was in my pocket, I shook my head.

'No.'

'*Passport!*' he repeated, a little more loudly. I shook my head again. I might have been reckless and intoxicated, but I wasn't giving my passport to anyone, and especially not the police in case I never saw it again. As smitten as I was with Prague, I preferred the option of leaving the country to remain available to me.

'You come police station,' one of them said.

'No.'

I'd like to think that if I hadn't been drunk, I wouldn't have climbed up on the statue in the first place, but I certainly wouldn't have had the balls to argue with such stony-faced policemen. The two men looked at each other, and one of them took out a small note pad and wrote on it, '10,000 K', which was the amount of Czech koruna they wanted me to pay as a bribe in lieu of a visit to police headquarters, the equivalent of about $500.

'No,' I said, like a broken record.

The policeman crossed out the first figure and wrote '5000 K'. I declined that offer, too, and the auction continued. Eventually the policeman wrote '1000 K' and underlined it twice. It was obviously his final offer, so I paid the bribe, fortunately the amount of money I happened to have left in my wallet, and walked back to my hotel, having discovered the market price for acting like a disrespectful turd in an Eastern European country.

I had originally planned to stay in the Czech Republic for a few days, but ended up staying for six weeks and would have stayed there forever if I could. I was afraid the way I felt would stop if I left; maybe there was something in the air, or the beer, although nobody else in Prague seemed as happy as I was. Misfiring brain chemistry aside, cigarettes were a dollar a pack and the Czech version of a cheeseburger is literally that – a crumbed, deep fried chunk of cheese in a white bun with a dollop of mayonnaise. Why would you *want* to be anywhere else?

The undiluted happiness evaporated so subtly, drop by drop, that I didn't notice it at first, but it gradually disappeared, as did my savings, when I moved on to Austria, Italy and France. Soon I was back in London with the same hollow feeling inside and no chance to remedy it with alcohol because I was faced with a sobering new challenge, to immediately find a job and somewhere to live or be reduced to eating from garbage bins and sleeping on park benches. It was almost summer but I was too chickenshit to sleep in a park, and garbage dining seemed a very hit-and-miss proposition.

Like so many of my impoverished countrymen and women before me, I picked up a *TNT Magazine* and began applying for 'live-in' positions, thereby hoping to kill two birds with one stone.

My first interview was at a pub in Islington, an inner-city area of London. The manager explained what the job would entail (predictably the exchange of money for beverages prepared by yours truly), and then gave me a tour of the staff living quarters. I followed him up a grubby, carpeted staircase to a dank, windowless lounge room that stank of stale smoke.

'This is the porn library. You can borrow whatever you want, just make sure you bring it back,' he said, pointing at a pile of dog-eared magazines and videos. 'And this is the communal stash bowl. We put all our weed in here and share it, and you're the only girl so don't leave any woman stuff in the bathroom over there,' he pointed in the direction of the slovenly amenities. 'There's six other lads living in and none of us wanna look at tampons and make-up and that.'

Given how much porn was in the room, and therefore a significant amount of 'woman stuff', the idea of concealing sanitary products and cosmetics from view seemed like a contradiction. Evidently my roommates were happy to see a woman's vagina, as long as the only thing going into it was a dick, or a couple of dicks, and not, god forbid, a tampon.

I felt uneasy for a couple of reasons, namely that the star feature of the staff accommodation was a 'library' of pornography and that I would be the only person with a vagina living among a bunch of misogynist stoners. And while I had no proof that my would-be roommates were rapists, the whole set-up felt a little rapey, so I headed back to the relative safety of the tube and homeless unemployment.

With a fresh wariness of London pub jobs, I turned to the 'Housekeeping' section of the *TNT* for other live-in options. I'd briefly worked as a maid at Club Med in the 'gap year' between dropping out of university for the first time and dropping out for the second. Living on a tropical island in far north Queensland sounded fun; cleaning hotel rooms on a tropical island, admittedly less so, but it beat working in a supermarket.

Arriving in paradise after three hours on a boat, fantasy collided with reality and came off second best, as it usually does. Disappointingly, living and working in a holiday resort wasn't anything like *Dirty Dancing*. Nobody was carrying a watermelon or arranging an abortion from a shady doctor and there didn't seem to be anyone on the island who could dance worth a damn. The only things being carried around by the employees were vacuum cleaners, mop buckets and hangdog expressions. The staff quarters resembled Portaloos fitted with beds and the honey trap was the staff bar, where you could put drinks on your 'tab', then find out just how many drinks you'd had when payday rolled around and most of your wages were missing.

It had happened long enough ago, though, for me to conveniently forget how crap it was when I found a house-keeping job advertised in *TNT*. I rang the hotel number and had the job one minute later, sight unseen. There was no mention of drugs or pornography, so it seemed like a step in the right direction.

Perhaps the eagerness with which I was hired should have rung some alarm bells, but I was desperate and even the ominous name of the place didn't deter me. According to the ad, I was going to be living in 'the heart of the Cotswolds', (whatever that meant) in a village called 'Upper Slaughter'.

★

The two-hour train trip from London to Gloucestershire was pleasant, past a patchwork of green and golden-brown fields and the sort of scenery I had only ever seen on the lid of a jigsaw puzzle, but I was nervous about what was waiting for me at the other end. I had no idea what to expect, and by the time the train stopped at Moreton-in-Marsh, my stomach was in knots.

The manager of the hotel met me at the train station and we drove down narrow country lanes in his boat of a Mercedes, making small talk about Australia and where I had travelled to in Europe. After twenty minutes, we turned on to a pebble driveway that crackled loudly under the wheels of the car and finally stopped outside an imposing seventeenth-century stone manor house that looked like something out of a television show where the butler did it. Surrounded by manicured gardens, hedges and a croquet lawn with cute black-faced sheep grazing in the distance, I felt like I'd fallen into a set from a British period film, except for the helicopter sitting incongruously on the far lawn. I asked the manager if it was his.

'No, it belongs to one of our guests. He often drops by to take afternoon tea in the garden,' he replied.

'Oh.'

So this was the kind of place where you took the *helicopter* if you felt like a scone and a cup of tea, presumably because your personal chef had been tragically kicked to death by one of the polo ponies that morning. I was in another world. When we went inside the beautiful hotel and I was handed two maid's uniforms, I was very aware of my assigned place in the British class system – at the bottom. Next, the manager escorted me to the staff accommodation across the road. On the outside it was another charming stone house with a peaked roof and a chimney, the sort of place that tourists come to England to take photos of, and I couldn't believe that I was going to be *living* in it. I immediately assumed that the interior of the building was going to be like the interior of the hotel, elegant and luxurious with lots of lovely antique furniture, but you know what they say about making assumptions – you come out looking like a massive dickhead. When we crossed the threshold and went indoors, my expectations took one sniff of the fetid air and promptly expired. A combination of stale cigarette smoke, beer and fermenting garbage greeted us and I made the mistake of looking down at the carpet, which was decorated with walked-in food and the filth of ages. My new home had a beautiful shell but it was ugly on the inside, like an apple with a worm in it or a model with a shit personality. My heart sank into my socks.

Up the stairs and down a narrow corridor, my bedroom awaited. Two double beds were wedged into opposite corners and I was introduced to a bespectacled French girl, who was smoking an unfiltered cigarette that smelt like a burning tyre. Her name was Frederique and she was my roommate. She shook my hand and said something in French that I didn't understand, so I just smiled moronically.

'I'll leave you to get settled in,' the manager said. 'Be at the hotel at seven tomorrow morning to have breakfast and start work at seven-thirty.'

'Okay. Thanks,' I replied, and then Frederique waved goodbye, too, and left for her dinner shift at the hotel restaurant where she worked as a waitress.

I sat down on my bed, feeling shell-shocked.

There was a bare light bulb hanging from the ceiling, with small flies buzzing wildly around it. The walls were covered in maroon striped wallpaper and Frederique, apparently a foodie, had torn pages from culinary magazines and stuck them all over the wall on her side of the room. The carpet was brown and filthy and covered in cigarette burns. I would never dare walk on it with bare feet, and I couldn't *wait* to see the bathroom. As expected, it was grotty, littered with strangers' pubes and the bathtub sported a thick ring of grime.

I decided to go for a walk, to get out of my dingy, rank-smelling house and explore Upper Slaughter before I gave in completely to despair. It took about ten minutes to see the whole village, five of which were spent sitting on a bench watching a stick float downstream in the river that trickled through the middle. Besides the hotel, there was a church, a cemetery, a handful of houses covered with ivy, a red telephone box, and *that was it*. I started to panic. I was in the middle of nowhere, with no money and no way out. There's nothing quite like feeling trapped, or *being* trapped, to make a mind even more ill at ease.

I went back to the room and tried on the blue and white striped maid's uniform I would have to wear in public in the morning. As expected, it was an unflattering sack guillotined at the waist with a frilly white apron that made me look like the 'before' photo in a Weight Watchers ad. I put it back on the hanger with a heavy heart and sat on the edge of my bed.

I glanced around the room, at the broken wardrobe, with one door hanging by a single hinge, the hideous uniform hanging inside it and the cloud of insects hovering above my head like an African halo. Feeling happy in Prague seemed like a lifetime ago, a dream, and this was the harsh reality that I had woken up to. The lump in my throat grew as I covered the stained mattress with clean sheets, and rolled my sleeping bag out on top for good measure. Then I lay down and cried bitterly, wishing that someone would come and rescue me or that a sinkhole would open up and swallow me. I just wanted to disappear.

The worst thing about Upper Slaughter wasn't the isolation, or that I had to walk three and three-quarter miles for essential supplies, or that I wasn't living in nearby Lower Slaughter, which at least had a place that sold cups of coffee. It wasn't even the fact that the hotel's promise of 'meals provided' meant leftovers or burnt scraps from the hotel kitchen that weren't fit to serve to paying customers, or that Frederique's decorating of our room with gastro-porn just reminded me how hungry I was all the time. Every one of those things paled to transparency compared with the grandeur of living in a house full of English chefs.

The sous-chef, Gavin, looked like a fat, blond version of Ricky Gervais and was forever adjusting his nuts and farting openly. I was the only female to arrive in the village in recent months with English as a first language and apparently Gavin had high hopes for me.

I met him on my second night in the house and his first words were, 'So we gunna do it, or what?'

I stared at him.

'That's my room over there,' he said, helpfully pointing to the door of his no-doubt pungent boudoir.

'Uh-huh, great,' I said, heading straight up the stairs to the relative sanctuary of my room. It was a shithole, but at least it was a shithole without Gavin in it, and the door had a working lock so I could ensure it stayed that way.

Another chef, John, a tall, lanky, brown-haired tree, called out after me, 'He'll think of yer when he's having a wank later!'

If I could have, I would have taken my brain out, placed it in a bowl and removed that image with soap and warm water, or steel wool and bleach if necessary.

After I'd been around for a few weeks and the novelty had worn off, I realised, with horror, that Gavin and the rest of the chefs had been on their best behaviour. By week three, every other sentence ended with, 'That's not what your mum said when I [*insert gross sexual act involving faeces or gargling of other body fluids*].' And it wasn't just Gavin farting like a draughthorse anymore, it was *all* of them. Our house smelt like a zoo.

For people who worked with food, the chefs had no interest in bringing their work home with them, except for the occasional hunk of foie gras pilfered from the hotel pantry. On those occasions, the foie gras (usually the size of a block of cheese) was fried in our only frying pan, eaten from the pan, and then left to congeal on the coffee table, next to empty beer bottles, chip packets and overflowing ashtrays. I never saw any of them wash their hands, ever, although I knew Gavin showered, because he liked to walk out of the bathroom with just a dirty towel wrapped around his waist, his doughy white body on display like a spectacularly unsuccessful one-man marketing campaign for a disgusting bakery.

Frederique said she was glad to be sharing a room with a native English speaker. She'd come to England to learn the language, but I didn't seem to be much of a teacher, perhaps because I'd never wanted the job in the first place. Whenever I asked Frederique if she liked something, she would always answer, 'Yes, very a lot.'

I explained to her, repeatedly, that you could like something *very much*, or like something *a lot*, but you couldn't say that you liked something *very a lot* because it didn't make sense. I gave examples to illustrate my point, 'I like fromage very much'; 'I like croissants a lot', but it didn't sink in.

'Do you understand?' I would ask her, hopeful that this time she might.

'Oui! Yes, very a lot!' she would reply, nodding her head enthusiastically.

So, Frederique was English-resistant, the chefs were animals and the rest of the housekeeping staff were various shades of weird, which I discovered because we had to work in pairs. The woman in charge was a maniac, a cleaning machine who did everything at breakneck speed and with frightening stamina, while her personality could most charitably be described as churlish. She drove the way she cleaned, too, and almost ran me over on a number of occasions tearing out of the car park at the end of her shift as if her house was on fire. It was exhausting to work with her and she showed no mercy to anyone who moved at a less frenzied pace, which was *everybody*. The usual extent of our workplace conversation was an irritated 'Hurry *up*!' followed by muttered expletives as she raced on to the next room while I was still only halfway through cleaning the first bathroom. I learnt not to take it personally. I was going to get paid whether I worked myself into a lather or not, and I'd never felt the urge to do so, not in Upper Slaughter or Club Med or anywhere else.

Another maid was an Egyptian woman who practically spat on the ground whenever she heard the words 'Israel', 'Jewish', or 'Netanyahu'. I made sure that the BBC News was never on television when we were cleaning a room together; invariably there would be mention of conflict in the Middle East and it would ignite a vitriolic rant that continued for the rest of the working day. She was open about her hatred of all Jewish people, but to be fair, she seemed to hate everybody else, too, and even inanimate objects like her cigarettes, which she furiously sucked to death. The only time I ever saw her smile was the morning she left in a taxi, leaving to go to her new job at a London hotel. I smiled back and waved goodbye, mouthing 'Mazel tov!' as she drove away.

Time passed slowly in Upper Slaughter. I crossed off each day on my handwritten calendar, wishing away the time until I was financially solvent and able to leave. I was bored, but resigned to my fate because unless I started laying golden eggs, I didn't have a choice. I smoked a lot of cigarettes, did a lot of writing, and all the walking and physical labour helped to keep any maudlin thoughts at bay for the most part. And unlike most of the other people I worked with, I knew that my placement was temporary.

As autumn set in, the local farmers began moving their sheep – the herds running clumsily through the street past our house, anxiously bleating and leaving a bunch of sheep shit and a lingering farm animal stink in their wake. For once the whole village smelt as bad as my house did. And, of course, it was the night after the sheep had passed through the village that I had insomnia and decided to call my parents from the red phone box across the road.

I should note here that I come from fainting stock. When I was seven, I had my tonsils removed and my dad came to visit me in hospital after the operation. He saw me being wheeled into the postoperative recovery room, unconscious on a trolley with tubes everywhere, and found the scene a little too gory for his tastes. He was almost at the front door when he fainted, hit his head on the floor and ended up in hospital with me for observation.

As I chatted to my mum in the dark, I began to feel strange and sort of groggy, probably because I was rapidly replacing the limited air supply inside the phone box with smoke.

'I feel a bit funny,' I told her, dropping a half-smoked cigarette to the floor and stamping on it, a gesture that was too little, too late for my oxygen-starved brain.

'What do you mean "funny"?' she asked, her concern palpable from the other side of the world, as my legs went weak and my vision became blurry.

'I think … I might faint,' I said vaguely.

'HANG UP THE PHONE! GO INSIDE. *QUICKLY!*' my mother yelled down the line.

'Okay,' I said weakly, barely managing to hang up the receiver through the descending mental fog. I took a couple of wobbly steps out of the phone box.

The next thing I knew, I was coming around, lying on my back in the middle of the street, in the middle of the night, in the middle of a pile of sheep shit. It was a definite low, but there had been so many that I wasn't sure where passing out in manure would place on the grand scale of my life. Feeling suicidal was at the furthest end, so I guessed this was somewhere between a break-up and a bad haircut. It occurred to me that I should probably moderate my use of tobacco, but I didn't. Cigarettes were my only friends in Upper Slaughter and if the prospect of emphysema and lung cancer wasn't deterrent enough to make me stop, fainting certainly wasn't going to cut it.

People often complain that there's 'nothing to do' where they live, even if they live in a town with a cinema and a bowling alley. In Upper Slaughter, there really *was* nothing to do. There weren't any mountains to climb, we didn't have a television and somebody stole the bicycle I'd borrowed from one of the other maids after I'd only had it a week. But there was one night that was truly exciting by Upper Slaughter standards.

Because the chefs were morons, they had moron friends, so our house was on permanent dickhead rotation and there were always people coming and going. Observing their interaction was the only source of entertainment on offer when I was tired of napping or reading books, and even though they were awful, I couldn't help myself. Their disgustingness was sort of marvellous, in a way.

One evening a new person arrived late for what typi-cally passed as a party at our place – sitting in the lounge room drinking cartons of beer after the restaurant kitchen had closed and smoking joints while slut shaming each other's mothers. As we lived in the middle of nowhere, the stoned, drunken chefs each assumed that the intense guy sitting in the corner was somebody else's friend, when in fact he was a lost stranger who had taken too many drugs in a field and stumbled towards the lights of our house in the dark. After twenty minutes of paranoid rambling, he abruptly left.

'Who was that knob?' Gavin asked, which was rich coming from him. Everybody shrugged.

'Dunno.'

'Ask yer mum, she's seen every knob in town,' John said, and with that, they were back to square one and it was revolting business as usual.

An hour later, the ordinarily mild-mannered, aristocratic boss of the hotel burst through the door and into the mushroom cloud of marijuana smoke.

'WHAT THE FUCK IS GOING ON HERE?' he roared. 'WHO CALLED THE FUCKING AMBULANCE?' Everybody froze.

Apparently the knob that *wasn't* Gavin had left our house and called an ambulance from the red phone box outside, claiming to be dying from a drug overdose. He had been taken to the nearest hospital, a forty-five-minute drive away, and the ambulance officers had notified the police, who had notified the hotel manager that the patient had come from our house, which was allegedly a drug den. And now the manager, furious and standing in a room that smelt like Snoop Dogg's Amsterdam holiday home, was looking for an explanation that was not forthcoming, having had the reputation of his fine hotel sullied by his employees. An ambulance turning up in the village to treat a drug overdose was the biggest scandal Upper Slaughter had ever seen, and news of it would spread like smoke. The chefs, usually so quick to say something smart (as in rude and sarcastic, not intelligent), stared at the floor as their hastily dropped joints burnt new holes in our squalid carpet. Nobody said a word. Gavin didn't even fart a reply.

'*FUCK YOU ALL!*' said the boss as he stormed out, violently slamming the door behind him. There was a brief catatonic silence, then a flurry of activity as the chefs scattered like cockroaches under a spotlight and began flushing all their contraband down the toilet. One of the chefs had a side venture selling hash, and all his merchandise disappeared down the pipes.

The police arrived early the next morning to raid our house and, testament to the previously unutilised cleaning skills of the chefs, 'nothing of interest' was found, a feeling I had come to know very well in Upper Slaughter.

After what felt like an eternity but was actually six calendar months, the time came to pack my bags and get the hell out of Gloucestershire, and I was surprised to find myself in tears. Unlike the first day, I wasn't distraught and wishing the earth would swallow me up so I could avoid what felt like a lengthy jail sentence in a maid's uniform. Instead there was a mixture of relief and joy, tempered by a decent amount of sadness that I hadn't anticipated experiencing. Upper Slaughter felt familiar and safe, and saying goodbye meant I lost those feelings, too. Maybe it was my customary contrariness, or Stockholm syndrome, but when leaving stopped being a dream and became a reality, I almost didn't want to go anymore. In spite of myself, I was comfortable there and it felt like my home, even if it was a filthy home where you had to wear shoes indoors for your own protection. It seemed that given sufficient time and an absence of other options, I could develop affection for anything. I would even miss Gavin a little.

Leaving was an emotional wrench, but my time there was over. It's only at the end that you can taste the bittersweet and feel a loss for things you never imagined you could miss. There are moments, sometimes, when I miss everything – my old school uniform, friends, past seasons and places that I didn't even enjoy at the time, the beginning of something that I'm at the end of. Sometimes I don't even know what I'm missing; there's just an indiscriminate longing for some small thing, everything, that I know is gone.

3   The Funny Thing About Depression

I love to laugh, and the funny thing about depression is … well, nothing, really. It's kind of like having a sense of humour lobotomy, and if I wanted one of those I would have found a job working in finance; people take cancer less seriously than money. I can't decide if it's worse, though, to have a shitty sense of humour (an attribute I gauge on viewership of shows like *Two and a Half Men*) than no sense of humour at all. Is it better to have no dog than half a dog? I suppose it depends on which half you get.

Nothing makes me cringe like unfunny people trying to be funny, but they're not entirely without charm. I give them credit for making up such a high percentage of the acts at open mic comedy nights, despite their impairment, and what they lack in comedic ability they seem to make up for with balls, delusion and an enviable thickness of skin. I like to think that those people are surrounded by a loving, supportive family and enthusiastic friends, who encourage them to go out and share their jokes with the world, even if their material is about as funny as child abuse. But what's *really* not funny is being unable to find the humour in anything, especially this ludicrous process we call life, where you're expelled from *another person's body* and then spend a large portion of your lifetime expelling unmentionables from your own.

Humour is precious to me, so there's a unique mortification attached to it falling flat or going horribly wrong that is matched only by other moments of humiliating awkwardness, such as walking around with the hem of my skirt tucked into my undies, or exiting the bathroom with a toilet paper tail. When humour goes right or occurs organically, magic happens, so depression really hits me where it hurts, right in the funny bone, which becomes just another nondescript bone in a morose skeleton.

When you're in a funk (a misleadingly fun-sounding way to describe a mood slump) you're far from the life of the party but at least you're not *alone* in it, even if it feels that way as you withdraw socially and in every other capacity and your existence can be most accurately compared to a house with its lights left on despite nobody being at home. According to the World Health Organization, 350 million people around the world have depression, so it's basically the McDonald's of mental illnesses – it's *everywhere*.

So the good news *and* the bad news is that there are a lot of other people out there who are also not having a good time, just like when I'm watching The Oscars on television. Worse news is that depression is known to be a major risk factor for suicide and almost one million people take their own lives each year, though at least this means that 349 million people are still hanging in there.

It's thought that depression has a genetic component that runs through a family tree, spoiling for a fight and seeking a vulnerability to exploit. My own family tree is strung with depression and other mental illnesses like garlands of tinsel at Christmas time, and, while not every branch has it, the tree unmistakeably glitters.

The Chambers side of the family, my dad's, but more specifically his mother's, offers a cornucopia of mental illnesses plus diabetes and male pattern baldness. My mother's side of the family features a variety of cancers, reflux and varicose veins. All in all this lavish genetic smorgasbord has options to suit most tastes. Please form an orderly queue to breed with me.

My mother, Clare, was a Moriarty before she married my dad and changed her surname to Chambers, so if you have any plans to steal my identity, I've just made it much easier for you (FYI, my bank account is currently not worth hacking, but I live in hope, so wait a few years). And while the Moriarty family may well have a colourful history when it comes to mental health, to the best of my knowledge no documentation exists to confirm or disprove this. As illustrated by my dad's rainfall logs and his habit of never deleting anything on his computer, however, the Chambers side of the family is quite keen on preservation.

My father, Andrew, is an all-or-nothing kind of personality and I'm like him in a lot of ways. We're both forgetful, creative, messy and have never met a short cut or a cheese we didn't like. And we've both had treatment for depression.

Obsessive in his interests, my dad's have included, at various times in his life, jogging (until he lost so much weight he looked like a whippet), cycling (until he was hit by a car for the third time and my mother made him stop), home brewing (in the end it was easier just to buy beer and it tasted better), maintaining a rain gauge (ongoing) and, at one stage, delving into our family history, something that yielded surprising news.

After his mother, Pat, died in 1997 my dad wrote to the epically named Department of Births and Deaths in South Australia, which provided him with a cache of information including birth, marriage and death certificates. Long-hidden skeletons came flying out of closets like it was freaking Halloween. One such skeleton was the death certificate of my great-grandmother Mary Ferguson, whose previously undisclosed cause of death, written in a neat and tidy hand, was 'Asphyxiation by drowning. Suicide.'

My grandmother Pat, Mary's daughter, had passed away at seventy after a lengthy illness, thought to be dementia or possibly Alzheimer's. Even as a child I can remember thinking that she often seemed nervous and worried, and I noticed that she fretted a lot about what other people thought and tended to minimise her own importance and wishes.

When she died I hadn't seen her for several years but I remembered the last time she had visited us, and how she had got lost just walking around the block. It had seemed harmless enough at the time, silly rather than cause for alarm, but the relentless mental deterioration that followed in the years afterwards turned her into a ghost. The person we had known growing up was no longer there. And it was Pat's side of the family whose unhappy origins could be found in the paper trail that led back to Edinburgh, Scotland, and to the Irvines and Millars who had preceded her.

Nobody is exempt from hardship and loss, even the Kardashians have lost a parent, but my great-great-grandmother Elizabeth Irvine, nee Millar, endured many. Her husband, Samuel Hanna Irvine, was killed in the First World War in France and a short time later, her brother John was also killed in battle, quite close to where her husband had died. Her surviving brother, William, a police constable in Leith, had migrated to Australia from Scotland in 1911, to the 'planned, free colony' of South Australia, a free settlement established without convict labour that focused instead on drawing skilled workers from Britain with various incentives. William began the long sea voyage by writing diary entries, sometimes several a day, but lost interest after two weeks, although not before he had shared his thoughtful, if politically incorrect, views from the Port of Algiers:

The Arabs are a dirty looking lot, none of them wear stockings and only a few wear shoes, and the men's garb, you can hardly tell whether it is trousers or petticoats.

William settled in Adelaide, and his newly widowed sister, Elizabeth, followed him to Australia in 1920 with her three children, Jess, Mary and Samuel. Presumably she was seeking a fresh start after the death of her husband and brother, and wanted to be near her remaining family.

Mary Irvine, my great-grandmother, was twelve years old when the family left Edinburgh and she kept a diary for the duration of the six-week, two-day sailing voyage, faithfully writing in it each day. It was the first time she had left Scotland and she was excited to be aboard the ship, describing the passengers' nightly moonlight concerts on deck and the activities undertaken to pass the time, like helping the cooks to peel potatoes and watching a tug of war between the British and the 'Colonials' that brought every passenger out of their cabin. The journey to Australia was an adventure for Mary. She saw flying fish darting across the water alongside the ship, the sun setting over the sea and striking scenery, but she was much less excited about the destination. She wrote grudgingly of it as 'the place with the horrid name of Adelaide – I feel sure I'm going to hate it. I would like to stay on board, and go straight back to Scotland.' If only the voyage hadn't had such an ominous shadow to detract from the fun.

Moving is a traumatic experience. When my family moved to Victoria from South Australia when I was ten, I remember being distraught after the first day at my new school and telling my parents that I wanted to go home, back to our old house, my old school and my friends in South Australia.

'You can't go backwards in life,' my mum had said. 'You can only go forwards.' I know that's true, but moving always feels like a little death and it doesn't matter how old you are. Severing ties with the home you know, even if it's for the greater good, hurts.

Mary's diary was well written, insightful and articulate, and there were also glimpses of a dry sense of humour. When discussing her difficulty trying to read a book in rough seas, a sarcastic sense of humour emerges that I suspect was genetically transferable.

I have been troubled to leave my place of resting no less than four times to pick up the precious book. Sleep I presume would be the most sensible thing – in my bunk – or perhaps on the floor.

She sounded like someone I would get along with, and she was twelve at the time. I can only imagine how well the diary I had kept as a twelve-year-old would have stood the test of time if I hadn't burnt it in the backyard when I was thirteen because I was already mortally embarrassed by the things I had written in it.

As the journey drew to a close, she wrote, 'Our happy (to me) voyage is nearing its end & for that reason I am by no means the happiest person on board.' And who could blame her? Even just reading her diary I started to feel anxious and dreaded the thought of her having to leave the boat to start a new life in a strange place. I wish she could have stowed away and gone on sailing the world forever. On 30 October 1920, her last entry read:

Like the burden of luggage I was carrying, my heart wasn't the lightest that went ashore from the faithful old ship. With Scotch company on board, one seemed to be just quite at home, but now staring at the black funnelled monster I realised how far I was from home, and that she was the only link between. I had to force back a silent tear as I thought of the six wonderful weeks, now gone for ever. I knew how dear the memory would be to keep and to cherish. Some may crave for the wide-open country in this land of many wonders, but nothing could ever fascinate me more than the beauties of the ever-changing sea, and such a life.

Mary, and the rest of the family, left the ship to begin their new lives in Adelaide, but it wasn't going to be smooth sailing there either.

Ten months after arriving in Adelaide, Samuel Millar Irvine, Mary's brother, had an 'attack' and 'threatened to drown himself'. His medical notes – all two A4 pages of them – were among the family archives, along with Mary's diary, and showed that seventeen-year-old Samuel was admitted to the Parkside Mental Hospital in June 1921. Formerly known as Parkside Lunatic Asylum until a change of name in 1913, the institution was more widely and informally known as 'The Bin', a place where people were discarded when nobody knew what to do with them, and that included unmarried women with children and prostitutes. Apart from one incident when he managed to climb over the fence and run away, Samuel went into the hospital and didn't come out again, dying there in 1932.

A picture of Samuel can be painted from his hospital notes, and it's a terribly sad, distorted Picasso with acne. The 'Important Facts' of his admission to hospital, an entry that accounts for one page of his medical record while his progress over the following *eleven years* is documented on the other page, states:

> *Patient has a vacant look. Cannot make himself under-stood. Wanders in his statements, has partial ideas centring round the sexual theme ... By mother, patient has not been sleeping much this last few nights ... Incoherent and irrelevant. Delusion that he has some venereal disease. He is 'afraid to look in a mirror'. Worried about religious affairs ... Says his illness is due to self-abuse. Loss of reasoning power.*

The scant collateral history provided by his mother, Elizabeth, describes Samuel as a loner who left school at fourteen years of age and had difficulty forming friendships. She states that he would occupy himself drawing in the evenings when he returned from his job as a warehouseman, but six months after arriving in Australia he 'began to be strange', becoming fixated with 'sexual matters'. His symptoms worsened over the next two months, to the point that Elizabeth had sought medical assistance.

Getting help for someone who was mentally ill in the 1920s meant that the men in white coats literally did come to take you away, whether you were agreeable to the plan or not, and, as the doctor had noted, Samuel 'on being restrained broke a window and tried to get out of the house'. He might have been delusional but he had sense enough to try to run.

Samuel's physical health was assessed as 'satisfactory' on admission to hospital with no abnormalities detected in his urinalysis or other physical observations, and in the section titled 'Family History', 'Mentally defective relative?' is raised as a possibility. The cause of the 'attack' is listed as 'Unknown' and the treatment prescribed? 'Rest in bed.' Lock him up and throw away the key doesn't have the same therapeutic ring to it, but that's what actually happened.

Samuel's hospital chart was updated once a month or so for the first year, and whenever something out of the ordinary happened, such as the episode in July 1922 when he climbed the fence and briefly escaped from the hospital grounds. Captured and returned to the hospital, he was 'Put back in No. 6', which sounds sinister and probably was. Other things deemed worthy of documentation were the occasional weight measurement and any episodes of loose bowel motions or onset of high temperatures that required him to be isolated to avoid an outbreak among the other thousand or so 'patients' who were locked up, too. Apart from that, the descriptions were mostly repetitive and brutally concise, 'Doing no good' and 'Going back mentally, very dull and stupid' and depict him wandering aimlessly through the hospital or unable to be roused from his bed, something I could relate to.

The entries, though sparse, show an obvious deterioration in his health. The boy who was 'clean in habits, eats and sleeps well' in the admission summary in 1921 became someone who was unable to maintain basic hygiene or feed himself two years later. In 1923, the chart states, 'No improvement whatsoever', which is pretty much the gist of all the entries, and the reports dwindle to six-monthly, then yearly, with nothing at all written in 1926 and 1929, which must have been particularly uneventful.

An infection that took hold in 1931 garnered seven chart entries, the most since the day of his admission, and the last entry, two months prior to his death in February 1932, reads, 'Temp up – pieces sent for culture'. The cause of death is stated as 'Enteritis, exhaustion'.

Samuel was finally out of the hospital; it just took him dying to make it happen. Sadly, he was born a couple of generations too early for the psychiatric medications that probably would have helped him and the antibiotics that would have saved his life, such as it was.

While Samuel was languishing in hospital, his sisters, Mary and Jess, grew up in the world outside, and at the age of eighteen Mary fell pregnant to a sailor called Jack Ferguson, a scandalous event. Elizabeth, a strict Methodist who wouldn't allow laughter in the house on Sundays, apparently disowned her daughter, as Mary's only contact with the family from that point on was via letter with her sister, Jess.

Jack and Mary were married in April 1927, aged twenty-three and eighteen respectively, and relocated to Melbourne, Victoria, where my grandmother Patricia Ferguson was born that September in Carlton. Sometime after that, they moved again, this time to Sydney, New South Wales.

As a sailor, Jack was often away from home for long stretches of time, and when he wasn't away at sea he could usually be found at the pub or the races, so I imagine he wasn't the greatest husband, or at least he was a husband who was reliably absent. Mary, at home alone with Pat, presumably had little other support available to her since she was estranged from her family and living interstate. It must have been quite a lonely existence, although the letter she had written to Jess two weeks before she died gave no indication that anything was amiss, stating that Jack was away at sea but due back in two weeks and 'Patty' was a lovely little girl who was always drawing.

A week before Pat's seventh birthday, and eighteen months after her brother, Samuel, died in hospital, Mary went to the beach and didn't come home again. She was twenty-five years old. An inquiry held in Manly in 1933 determined that the cause of death was suicide by drowning, but there was no other information available about the inquiry's findings or the circumstances of her death, such as the whereabouts of Jack and Pat. Whatever the details were, suicide was the only course of action Mary could see for herself.

Pat was taken back to Adelaide to be cared for by her grandmother. Elizabeth, having lost a husband, a brother, and now two of her children in short succession, one from madness, the other from suicide, inherited a child who had effectively lost both parents when Jack disappeared to Darwin. It's presumed that he was forbidden from having any contact with Pat, because it wasn't until Elizabeth died that Jack was back in Adelaide to see her. Pat was thirty-seven by then, married and with children of her own. It had been thirty years since they'd seen each other.

I remember Jack. He was a nice man who was never without a cigarette, a habit resulting in the emphysema that eventually killed him, and he always had butterscotch lollies in his caravan that he would let us kids help ourselves to, which we considered a fine quality in an adult. We didn't see him very often, but he was a familiar face, someone who turned up occasionally and had been doing so for as long as we could remember. We had no inkling of his lengthy absence or the turbulent history of which he had been a part.

Pat always said that her mother had died from a 'septic throat', because that's what she was told, and she never found out that her mother committed suicide. The people who knew what had really happened, presumably Jack, Elizabeth, and Jess, had kept it a secret. And nobody would ever have known if Mary's death certificate hadn't arrived in the mail. When it surfaced, it explained a lot, and both comforted and frightened me.

★

A few years ago, my dad was admitted to hospital for treatment of his severe depression. It had developed progressively, in tandem with a lot of stress, in his fifties until it eventually became overwhelming, whereas the onset of my depression was quite abrupt and occurred in my teens.

Because I could relate to what he was going through, I thought that I would naturally be a great support to my dad, but depression looks very different from the outside. Despite the best of intentions, I found my empathy wilting faster than the flowers in his room. When *you're* in it, you can't shake it, but when you're around someone else who's in it, you want to shake *them*. It's patently unfair, but depression is a deeply unattractive illness, especially when people don't recover in a timely fashion, and they rarely do. Usually, it's a long road. When someone you love is stuck in the mire of depression, your sympathy wears out after a while, chewed up by impatience as your concern warps into frustration. When you're on the outside looking in, all of the well-meaning, ultimately futile things people say when you're depressed, like, 'Cheer up! Look on the bright side! Things could be worse! You could be starving in Africa! Snap out of it! Think positive!' come to your own mind just as easily, and sometimes escape your mouth, too. If it were that easy to get over depression, there wouldn't be any. It's a cruel illness and all you can do is wait for a change and hope for the best.

I was lucky in that I responded well and relatively quickly to medication, and also because it was the first medication I tried. My dad wasn't so fortunate. He tried a succession of antidepressants, enduring side effects for weeks as the dose of each was gradually titrated to a 'therapeutic level', and then, when the drug didn't help, weaned off it in order to try the next one. It was a protracted and expensive process, which would have been tolerable if any of the medications had been even a tiny bit effective, but besides plain not working, the medications also resulted in numerous unpleasant side effects, including facial tics, sedation, and facial numbness that made him drool, and practically extinguished the small, remaining spark of his personality.

The simple things that promote wellbeing (and counter depression and anxiety), such as eating well, exercising and getting enough sleep, are often the first things to fall away as you begin to slide into the abyss, creating additional momentum. My dad lost interest in swimming, something he used to do every morning that obviously helped to alleviate his stress, and his misery snowballed from there. His energy levels were low, and stayed low. Grocery shopping and preparing any kind of food was a huge effort, eating was reduced to a chore and if left to his own devices he would have slept all day. You're alive, but you can't really call it living.

Entrenched in his depression, we badgered him to at least go swimming again, but he couldn't bring himself to do it until he had started to feel a bit better. And then he did, which made him feel a tiny bit happier, and his energy levels were resuscitated, which meant he took more interest in his diet. When it changed direction, the vicious circle was helpful.

In all, it took a long time for him to recover, about two and a half years from the start, but thankfully the depression resolved by itself, and it did so in spite of all the attempted pharmaceutical interventions. My dad and I had the same sort of illness but very different responses to medication because brains are like snowflakes, big, ugly, grey snowflakes, and no two are the same.

I used to be very sensitive about the word 'crazy' because I was afraid I actually might be. It hit a nerve. I still have my moments, but I think it's just residual paranoia. Before I began taking medication I once confessed my fear to my sister, and clarified that I didn't mean the jumping-into-a-swimming-pool-with-all-your-clothes-on kind of crazy.

'Crazy people don't know they're crazy, so you're not crazy,' she'd told me at the time, but I sure didn't *feel* not crazy. I might not have been hearing voices or seeing things, but I felt overwhelmed and miserable and didn't understand what was happening to me or why it wouldn't go away. And once a month I felt even worse.

While I may have a grip on the depression thing now, premenstrual syndrome is real, people, and it still wants me to have a terrible time for several days each month. This means that I spend around ten weeks a year, on average, feeling as emotionally volatile as a toddler, but since the alternative to PMS *is* a toddler, I'll take the PMS (thankfully, medication really helps with that, too). I'm fairly certain that the reason I've never felt compelled to have a child is nature's way of preventing another Sylvia Plath situation – a prolonged period of sleep deprivation, not to mention everything else that comes with a baby, would probably end up with me sticking my head in an oven as well.

Despite my history, if it comes up in conversation that I take medication for depression, people are often surprised.

'But you always seem so happy!' they exclaim.

Yes, I am, mostly. Zoloft really helps to make that happen for me. But sometimes my thoughts and feelings are unbearable, even on medication, and the only thing I can do is wait it out, or speed up the process by crying, walking or lying in the bath with the lights off. 'It's a cloud, it'll pass,' I tell myself, but sometimes the cloud is as heavy as an anvil. I have to wait for that hateful little hamster turning on a wheel in my brain to become exhausted and stop for a while. Like Robert Frost says in his poem of the same name, 'Nothing gold can stay,' and while it may seem like a depressing sentiment, I personally find it incredibly heartening. Everything leaves eventually, and if the gold can't stay forever, then neither can the darkness.

When I'm feeling happy, I sometimes think to myself that living with depression isn't so bad, but it's the kind of thing I say when I've forgotten how it feels. And when I am reminded, and it seems that I will be reminded periodically for reasons unknown or only to be guessed at, I can't believe there was ever a minute of happiness in my life. If it weren't for the photos – the proof that at times I've had more reason to smile than many – I would swear it wasn't true. So I feel a lot of sympathy for my deceased relatives, for my grandmother Pat, her mother, Mary, and uncle, Samuel, none of whom had the option of medication, or even a language for what was happening to them. Being born in the 1970s meant I had a much better chance of finding a treatment option that didn't involve being imprisoned and abandoned, and distanced me from suicide. I'm extremely grateful for that.

4 Six Million Dong

In 2001 I'd returned to Australia from England, thoroughly sick of jobs I didn't give a crap about. So I spent the next three years studying to become a nurse, paying for my food and rent with more jobs I didn't give a crap about, but which helped me to keep my eye on the prize – a rewarding career that paid more than peanuts and didn't make me want to kill myself. Nursing was it, and the first holiday my new career enabled me to take was to Vietnam in 2005 with my best friends, Rachell and Rachael (I have a type).

The three of us had bonded as poor student housemates and were now ready to enjoy the fruits of our labour. Rachell was a psychologist and Rachael worked at a travel agency – her proximity to glossy international travel brochures inspiring us to holiday overseas. However, we didn't select Vietnam as our destination because we wanted to appreciate how charmed our lives were or because we had questions about the country's culture and its traumatic history (that would have made us look like better people).

We chose Vietnam because we thought it would be interesting, we liked Vietnamese food and because we were collectively woeful at saving money, electing to immediately dispose of most of our disposable incomes on nights out and new clothes. Vietnam was one of the only places we could afford to visit. Our timing was impeccable. 'Bird flu' was all over the news, and my mother pleaded with me not to 'touch any chickens' while I was away. I assured her that this would not be an issue.

When we arrived in Ho Chi Minh City, after an overnight flight from Brisbane via Singapore, the usual tedium ensued: passport inspection, baggage collection and a stop at an ATM to withdraw some local currency. I was impressed to discover that even after a substantial withdrawal my savings account contained six million dong. Although I was thirty years old, displaying maturity in the face of a currency called the dong, not to mention place names like Phuc Long Hotel or Fuking Restaurant, was never going to happen. We laughed like drains the entire holiday.

The culture shock began before we'd even left the arrivals area, when a large group of men started shouting at us, pleading with us to take their taxi to our accommodation and crowding around us like we were The Beatles.

'Taxi? Taxi? You nee hotel?'

Rachael and I looked at each other; we were sleep-deprived, bewildered by the sudden humidity, and overwhelmed by being yelled at by an unanticipated crowd of strangers. The other Rachell, however, took it in her stride.

'Follow me,' she said, walking purposefully out of the airport building. 'I've got this.'

We trailed meekly behind her as she began to negotiate with the jostling drivers who yelled prices at her like it was an auction, which it sort of was.

'You use the meter?' she asked, and several of the drivers shook their heads, offering her a 'special' fixed price instead.

Rachell had travelled to India after she had finished high school, and to say she hadn't enjoyed it would be like saying that the *Titanic* didn't really enjoy smooth sailing, but her terrible experiences there *had* endowed her with the ball-busting wisdom required to negotiate with Vietnamese taxi drivers. Rachael and I were deadweight during the brokering and would happily have paid any inflated price as long as people stopped yelling at us and took us to some place with airconditioning.

Rachell pointed at one guy, who nodded eagerly in response to the meter demand. 'Okay, you use the meter, we'll go with you.'

He seized the backpack from her shoulder and led us to his taxi before she could change her mind.

When our luggage was in the car, Rachael and I nervously hugged our backpacks to our chests in the back seat while Rachell sat in the front, and immediately got into an argument with the driver, who had started to drive off *without* turning the meter on.

'Turn the meter on,' Rachell instructed.

'Me-er broken,' he said, shrugging.

'If you don't turn the meter on, we're not going to pay you,' she replied.

He shook his head again, vigorously this time. 'No work! Broken!'

Rachell wasn't buying it. She spoke coldly, so coldly in fact that my blood would have frozen to ice if she'd been talking to me. 'Stop the car,' she said. 'We're getting out.'

The driver looked at Rachell. Meanwhile, Rachael and I looked at each other and began to slide down into our seats like a couple of amoeba, recoiling from the confrontation. We had driven about ten metres in total, apparently one of the more awkward distances.

It was a Vietnamese stand-off as the driver sized up Rachell and she met his gaze with the cool intensity of a serial killer. He turned the fully functioning meter on with a scowl, and we finally left the airport car park.

The next battle was getting the driver to take us to the cheap hotel in the middle of the city that we had booked online. Rachell told him the name of the hotel, showed him the address she had written down, and he shook his head.

'No, no! Hotel bur dow! I take you, special price, very *niii* hotel!' he said, eager to help. How unfortunate that our hotel had burnt down in the three days since we'd made the booking. It was unbelievably bad luck.

Rachell was completely unfazed.

'No,' she said calmly, 'you take us to our hotel or no money. *No dong!*'

He didn't say anything after that.

However, the little meter drama was *nothing* compared with the rest of the drive into Ho Chi Minh City. Cars, motorbikes, buses, trucks, bicycles, pedestrians, rickshaws and carts all converged on the road in a chaotic cacophony. It was the most terrifying experience of my life, until I got out of the car and had to cross the street on foot. When a motorbike is flying at you, often with three or more people balanced upon it, your first instinct is to run, but apparently this is the worst thing you can do because it doesn't give the oncoming traffic a chance to swerve around you, if they should be so inclined. In spite of what I'd been told (stride purposefully, but DO NOT RUN) I walked a little too briskly, holding my breath and praying to baby Jesus that I'd make it to the other side without being mowed down.

Why did the chicken cross the road?

It's where the hotel was, or I wouldn't have.

Taking everything for granted is something that we Richie Richs in wealthy first-world countries do exceptionally well. We tend to look at our car, clothes and homes and think longingly of the better version that we know is out there because we saw it featured in a magazine or on television. The pursuit of the bigger, brighter, newer, faster – pick an adverb, any adverb – fuelled by advertising, the media and greed, consumes us. We're 'glass half empty' thinkers. For example, if we're given a glass of milk, we'll gripe that it's not organic, suitably chilled or derived from

almonds, or that we can tell just by the taste that the cow it
came from wasn't smiling at the time it was being milked,
and now our day is *ruined*.

I don't know anyone who says Grace or gives thanks
before a meal, although I have a vague recollection of doing
so when my brother, sister and I were kids, as well as using
our forks as crude slingshots to stick peas to the ceiling
whenever our parents left the room. As adults, we may
thank the person who physically puts the plate on the table,
but we expect the food to be there. We *expect* everything,
even when we already have it.

Ho Chi Minh City was an eye-opening experience.
Sometimes I wanted to scrunch my eyes shut and never
open them again, like when I saw cages full of cute puppies
for sale and realised they were for eating, not cuddling, and
when a three-year-old boy tried to sell us cigarettes and
chewing gum in a bar at two in the morning. His mother
stood outside, waiting to take him to the next bar filled
with drunken tourists.

The power lines in the city streets hung like gnarled
vines, tangling around the power poles like Silly String,
and looked even more dangerous than the traffic below,
which was saying something. It was incredible that the
entire city hadn't burnt to the ground, let alone that such
an insane spaghetti of wires could viably carry electricity.

We had been told that the War Remnants Museum was
a 'must see' while we were in Ho Chi Minh City, and it
wasn't like other museums I'd been to. There was nothing
subtle about it; our visit was horrifically educational. The

first display we saw was a glass cabinet housing jars of preserved human foetuses, with gnarled deformed bodies illustrating the devastating results of exposure to Agent Orange in utero. A nearby wall was hung with the photos of children who had survived gestation, but who had been born without eyes or with features that were grotesquely distorted, like a terrible cartoon drawing come to life, and limbs that were thin and withered or entirely absent. And it wasn't just the birth defects that were heartbreaking, but the bleak background of the photos, the children lying in cots in hospitals that they would probably never leave, or sitting alone in an empty room with barred windows. You could leave the museum, but the images followed you out, to the beggars who sat outside the marketplace with hands outstretched, and faces and bodies so deformed they looked like they were made from melted plastic.

The poverty and hardship, en masse and up close, made me think about my depression and stirred up the guilt I always felt about being 'sad' when I had nothing, comparatively, to be sad about. I came from a country with a lot of material wealth and a sense of entitlement where happiness was concerned. But what if I had been born into poverty and my focus was on my day-to-day survival? What would depression look like then? Would I have bigger fish to fry and no time to think about how I felt? Was it an affliction of the privileged? Maybe the price of having your basic needs met was a perverse dissatisfaction with life, like worrying about getting fat now that you had stopped worrying about finding something to eat.

There was no way of knowing, really. And no matter what was happening in my life externally, the depression had always been there, fortunately inactive for large swathes of time. Feeling guilty about its presence – something I had as much control over as the colour of my eyes – was like breaking my leg and then berating myself for not running a marathon. But at least a broken bone makes sense. Being sad for no reason does not.

It was monsoon season. The weather had been unchangeable, oppressively humid, hot and sunny, the air heavy with smog and the smell of percolating garbage, but on our last day in Ho Chi Minh City we were baptised by nature. Rachell, as ever the most prepared, had thought to pack an umbrella, but Rachael and I had not. When a sudden storm rolled in, dumping torrential rain as we were out walking around the city, it took about ten seconds for us to be soaked to the skin. Rachell had the upper hand for a minute, until her umbrella blew inside out and turned into a piece of trash. We bought rain ponchos from a street vendor, even though we were already wet, and sloshed back to the hotel through dirty street water as the drains were punished to overflowing, laughing hysterically at each other wearing what looked like full body condoms.

After Ho Chi Minh City, we travelled north by train in a sleeper cabin to the coastal hub of Nha Trang. The train was far from the glamorous *Orient Express* experience I'd hoped for (my imagination is tenacious) but it was passable, though cramped, with two triple bunk beds jammed into a very small space. We slept most of the way there, and far more important than restricted space was the fact that we managed to not roll off our bunks in the dark, avoiding a guaranteed spinal injury as a memento of our holiday.

The monsoon storms had beaten us to Nha Trang, and the beach, usually one of the city's main drawcards, was a brown washing machine of foamy, turbid water. Our first glimpse of the shoreline included a man who stood with his back to us, pissing into the surf, which pretty much set the mood for our stay.

Employing a reckless, uneven method of accommodation selection, we picked places that either had a name we thought was funny or a good review from the Lonely Planet guide, categories that often didn't overlap. When we opened the door to our room at the *Hotel O-Sin* we were bowled over by a strong, musty smell emanating from a dubious-looking carpet. The plastic slippers in the bathroom, intended for use in the shower, were covered in black mould. If they came *with* mould, then what kind of super-fungus were they supposed to be shielding us from? I shuddered to think.

'There are toadstools growing in this corner,' Rachell called out. Hotel O-Sin was more like 'Hotel O-Syphilis'. That's what we got for being flippant about our choice of lodging.

The sky was grey and overcast, but our room was repellent enough to get us outdoors and up to a beautiful hilltop temple that provided sweeping views over Nha Trang. It was pretty, if flooded in areas, but it was a beach city and this was definitely not beach weather. We walked around aimlessly for the rest of the day and then went back to our hotel. It had a bar/restaurant (plastic tables and chairs that looked out on to the street) and we drank beers into the evening, waving away persistent street vendors who tried to sell us bags of sliced fruit and Zippo lighters bizarrely adorned with a smiling Saddam Hussein portrait.

A summit was called as night descended and since none of us were willing to sleep in our mouldy room and the weather was rubbish, we decided to cut our losses. We paid for the room, and twice as much for all the beers, then went back to the train station and splashed out on 'first class' train tickets to Hoi An, ready to be embraced by luxury.

Naively, we had imagined that a first class train ticket would equal something fancy by Western standards, but by Western standards, it was perhaps the equivalent of first class in jail. Our cabin had two bunk beds with thin mattresses that looked like they had been gnawed on by animals and were littered with other people's hair, cigarette burns, a couple of butts, petrified chewing gum, ash, oil stains and other mysterious blemishes.

Rachell is a very kind-hearted person but possesses a cutthroat sense of justice. After we'd all drunk numerous beers, she was the first to explore the train's bathroom options and reported back: 'It's a squat toilet, and it's gross.'

Rachael and I wailed in protest, and held out for as long as possible before grudgingly submitting to the call of nature. Rachael went first, and came back trembling. And then it was my turn to become acquainted with the half-inch thick layer of sludge covering the entire floor as I tried valiantly to avoid slipping over on a moving train with my pants around my ankles. When I got back to our carriage, which suddenly seemed a lot less disgusting, I wanted a shower but as there wasn't one I took out a bag of alcohol wipes I'd stashed in my bag. We obsessively disinfected our hands and feet and any other area of skin that had made contact with the surface of the bathroom. And then Rachell spoke up, 'There's a Western toilet at the other end of the carriage, but I didn't realise until after I used the squat toilet and if I had to use it, then so did you.' She broke up laughing.

That bitch.

We erred on the side of caution and assumed that the bedding provided had never been washed. To avoid touching the mattresses, we zipped ourselves into our sleeping bags, right up to our necks, and the plastic rain ponchos came in handy again, this time as hygienic pillow-cases. A 'meal' was provided, but as it consisted of tripe and rice, we ate Pringles instead. We ate so many fucking Pringles on that trip I still don't want to eat them nine years later.

The other feature of our cabin, common to every train carriage we travelled in, was a corner speaker blaring nonstop Vietnamese folk music. It didn't have a volume control knob, or an off switch, and we could still hear the music clearly through our earplugs, even when we pushed them in so far they almost touched our brains. It felt like the train was trying to break us.

Hoi An was the lovely reward for our insalubrious train ride. We stayed at a place with a comforting name, Thahn Binh III Serene Hotel, a swimming pool and a breakfast buffet, and wandered around the pretty historical town feeling like we had stumbled into a quaint paradise. A former port situated by the river, it had beautifully preserved buildings, colourful food markets and several French patisseries we descended upon like vultures. Even walking across the street didn't feel like a kamikaze act. The streets were full of tailors' shops where you could have any clothes or shoes you wanted custom-made and we went berserk, ordering silk tops and jackets that were so perfectly cut that they no longer fitted if we ate a meal or drank a glass of water.

Bitten once, and twice shy, we took a bus from Hoi An to Hue, the next city on our itinerary, and while there was no squat toilet issue, there was a very annoying American girl who was similarly full of shit. She would *not* shut up. Exchanging stories, information and cautionary tales with people you meet while travelling is usually entertaining, and often helpful, but occasionally you meet a jerk who wants to turn it into a contest and can't sense your disinterest.

'What countries have you been to?' the American asked.

'Just this one,' Rachael answered. 'We're spending two weeks in Vietnam.'

'Oh,' she said, clearly unimpressed. If we had reeled off a list of countries, each more exotic and far-flung than the last, she would have had somewhere better or more remote to top it. And if we wanted to hurt her feelings, all we had to do was call her a tourist. She would have practically immolated herself to escape the stigma.

'So, you're not going to Cambodia?' she asked.

'No,' I replied.

'You totally should,' she said. 'It's *really* poor, so it's super-cheap. It's great.'

I produced my trusty earplugs and feigned sleep for the rest of the journey, even though there was actually no chance of falling asleep as the bus driver leant on the horn and swerved around trucks, motorbikes and pedestrians, narrowly missing every one. Keeping my eyes shut served two purposes: thwarting the chatty American and protecting myself from traumatic shock.

After a couple of pit stops, we arrived in Hue. As soon as we stepped out of the bus we had to fight our way through a crowd of men who pawed at us, trying to get us to stay at their hotels. I didn't mind being yelled at but I didn't like being touched and, already irritated by the American, I lost my temper, screaming, 'FUCK *OFF*!' at the top of my lungs. The crowd, startled by my abusive outburst, fell away and we started walking. The American girl trailed behind us, dragging a suitcase on wheels, which was *also* incredibly noisy, and completely impractical in a country where footpaths were either nonexistent or a succession of giant potholes interspersed with piles of rubble and bricks. She tried to persuade us to join her at the cheap accommodation in Hue that she'd been told about.

'*It's two dollars a night!* Can you believe it? I *love* this country!' she exalted.

The places we had stayed in were around twenty dollars per night for the three of us. There was *no fucking way* we were staying anywhere that cost two bucks. We parted ways at the next street corner, wished her well but didn't mean it, and as we walked off in opposite directions, no longer hearing her annoying voice was one of the simple highlights of my holiday. The only thing that could top it was a massage, and that was something we planned to find in Hue.

A massage is a luxury anywhere, but in Australia it's an expensive luxury. In Asia it's much more affordable, although the language barrier creates more potential for miscommunication, mixed messages and resultant awkward weirdness.

After we had checked out the major tourist attraction of Hue, the Citadel, and eaten some pho, a kind of noodle soup, we were ready for some pampering. We enquired about 'spa treatments' at a big hotel by the river, a few blocks from where we were staying in our budget accommodation. They offered a massage service and the price was as cheap as any we had seen elsewhere so it was a done deal. Each of us was spirited away to a separate room by a masseuse in a very short white uniform. I was looking forward to the wonderfully relaxing massage that surely awaited.

My masseuse hovered somewhere between unfriendly and businesslike.

'You undress, no clothe,' she ordered.

'Take off *all* my clothes?' I asked, unsurely.

'Yeah,' she replied.

'Including underwear?' This was the part that I felt needed clarification.

'Yeah! All, *all*!' she said impatiently, handing me a towel before she left the room.

I felt nervous about getting *completely* nude for a massage, but what did I know? This was my first massage at a spa in Vietnam. 'It must be how it's done here,' I thought. So I undressed, put my clothes, shoes and bag on the chair in the corner of the room, then climbed up on to the white plastic-topped table, unsure how to best position myself. I had expected there to be a hole in the table to put my face in, but there wasn't, so I lay on my back and covered as much of myself with the tiny, thin towel as I could. It left very little to the imagination, but that didn't matter because as soon as the masseuse returned to the room, which had the bright fluorescent mood lighting of a supermarket and remained on for the duration, she reefed the towel away and dropped it on to the table next to me.

I lay there naked, feeling very insecure. The massage was off to a bad start, and it got a whole lot worse when she poured oil all over my chest and stomach, climbed up on the table, straddled me and proceeded to aggressively knead me all over like I was a pile of dough. I've never felt so tense in my life. This was not the aromatherapy, dimly lit, soothing interaction I had in mind, it was bread making on a Slip 'N Slide. I shut my eyes and hoped it would end quickly.

It didn't.

'Turn, turn!' she barked at me and I rolled over on to my front with great difficulty now that half of my skin was coated in oil. My face pushed into the plastic as she jumped on my back like a deranged jockey. I was only at the halfway mark. Oh god.

A good massage never lasts long enough. It seems like time speeds up and that you've only been there for five minutes when the alarm goes off, or the masseuse gently tells you that your session is over and offers you green tea or a glass of water. A bad massage, conversely, seems to go on forever, like a long, bitterly cold winter.

'*You dress!*' she snapped, when the massage mercifully ended after what felt like three weeks. I dressed hurriedly, feeling a mixture of shame, embarrassment and extreme greasiness. I wasn't sure what had just happened but it appeared to lie somewhere between a lap dance and an assault. Really, it all boiled down to being sans pants. If I had been wearing underwear, it still wouldn't have been the massage I was after, but it wouldn't have felt *quite* as wrong or as uncomfortably close to accidental sex tourism.

After I had paid the woman at the front desk for my 'spa treatment', a hefty tip built into the price, I went out to the poolside area where Rachael and Rachell were waiting, drinking coffee and looking perturbed. Rachell was smoking a cigarette intensely, in a way that looked medicinal rather than recreational.

'Was your massage really ... *weird*?' I asked them.

'I think I just got date-raped,' Rachell said, exhaling deeply. Rachael nodded in agreement.

'Oh, thank god, I thought it was just me!' I said, relieved. 'You had to get completely naked, too?' I asked, and they looked at me strangely.

'What do you mean *completely* naked?' Rachell asked, confused. 'Without your *underwear* on?'

'Yes! She told me to take off all my clothes, including my underwear!' I replied. 'Didn't you?'

'*NO!*' they both exclaimed. 'You were *naked* for that? OHMYGOD! That's *so* much worse!'

And my alleged best friends laughed their heads off.

Although we had bitched incessantly about the trains, they weren't bad enough to deter us from taking one from Hue to Hanoi for the last substantial leg of our journey. We were beginning to get used to things in Vietnam but, as always, we had a stash of Pringles, bottled water and plastic ponchos on hand.

We arrived in Hanoi early in the morning, just as the sun was rising, and had the usual battle of wills with a taxi driver who agreed to take us to our hotel in the Old Quarter of the city. The streets were eerily quiet and empty, save for a lone woman squatting over a shopping bag by the side of the road, her skirt in a bunch over her knees.

'Sorry,' the driver said.

'At least she's doing it in a bag,' Rachell said. 'I do *not* miss India.'

When we got to our hotel, there was a sizeable cock-fighting rooster strutting outside the front door, a last feathery hurdle between us and a much-needed shower, and as per the conditions of the pre-existing parental agreement, I didn't touch it.

Like most travellers to Vietnam, we took advantage of our proximity to cheap goods, such as the Adidas sneakers I loved that were actually made there. In addition to pirated DVD box sets, Rachael and Rachell had stocked up on packets of apricot facemasks and decided to indulge in some restorative grooming at the hotel before we went out to look around Hanoi. I lay on my bed and read a book while they tied their hair back, spread the gooey concoction over their faces and waited for it to dry.

After a few minutes, Rachell said, with difficulty, 'My face feels really tight.'

'Mine, too,' Rachael mumbled. 'Maybe we've left it on too long.'

They checked the discarded packets for instructions and found them unhelpfully written in Vietnamese. However, the ingredients were listed in English, and turned out to be 'glue' and 'apricot flavor'. Rachell and Rachael screamed, albeit in a muffled way, and ran to the bathroom to wash their faces while I laughed. Their complexions may not have been transformed in a positive way, but if anyone broke a shoe or decided they wanted to start sniffing glue, we had the means.

On the surface, Hanoi seemed a little less gritty and chaotic than Ho Chi Minh City. There was a pretty tree-lined lake in the middle of the city and stately French colonial buildings amidst the pastel Vietnamese-style houses. The traffic was still mental, but as we entered the cool green oasis and sat by the edge of the lake, it felt a long way from the city. And then a syringe floated by …

The tangled power lines in Hanoi were just as wild and unruly as those in Ho Chi Minh City, but had old-fashioned loudspeakers peeking out from them on busy street corners. Relics of the war, the speakers had been used to broadcast warnings of imminent bombing, and were now used to give 'information' to Hanoi's citizens and to play rousing anthems. We had no idea what was actually being broadcast during their twice-daily trumpeting, so it was easy to imagine Communist propaganda falling on our deaf ears, and that we had travelled to another time and not just to another country.

Like many other experiences in Vietnam, the coffee situation was intense. When you asked for coffee at a café, it came in a small metal coffee filter resting on top of your glass. The black coffee dripped through the base, settling on top of a layer of condensed milk. Once the brewed coffee was stirred into the sweet milk, it became caramel-coloured liquid *crack*, a potently eye-opening, caffeinated sugar hit. We were addicted after the first two days, so much so that we went to the supermarket in Hanoi looking for bags of coffee and pots to take home with us to maintain our habit.

Finding a shelf stacked with bags labelled 'Weasel' coffee, we figured it was just a silly name or perhaps an error in Vietnamese–English translation, but then a Canadian backpacker standing nearby helpfully explained it to us.

'It's called Weasel coffee because the beans get eaten by weasels, ferment in their gut, and then they're pooped out and turned into coffee. I guess they just wash the poop right off … It tastes much better than you'd expect when you know it's been through a weasel, right?' he said, smiling.

We thought he was joking, at first, and laughed a little awkwardly. And then we realised that he was an earnest Canadian who was telling us the truth, however disturbing. We learnt something uncomfortable about ourselves that day: we liked the way a weasel's ass tasted, because apparently we had been drinking coffee that had come out of one for ten days straight. There didn't seem much point in stopping now, so we bought two bags of Weasel and a drip coffee pot each, but it was never the same when we drank it at home because the noisy, stinky essence of Vietnam was missing.

The Old Quarter of Hanoi was crowded with travel agencies peddling day trips and sightseeing deals to tourists like us, so we decided to go on a 'junk boat' trip to Ha Long Bay and Cat Ba Island in our last days. The pictures in our Lonely Planet guide were impressive and after a hair-raising three-hour ride in a minibus, and more Pringles, we made it to the boat harbour unscathed. The junk boat was beautiful, with lots of ornate dark wood and intricate carvings, and wasn't actually *constructed* of junk, as I'd feared it might be.

Maybe it was the crack coffee I'd been drinking, but for me Ha Long Bay should have been called 'How Long Bay' or maybe 'How Much Longer Do We Have to Look at These Limestone Cliffs Bay' (answer: four hours). I took a bunch of photos of the towering limestone cliffs as we sailed out into the bay, but after twenty minutes of gawking and taking what looked like the same photo over and over, I was bored and restless. Luckily, on-board video entertainment was thoughtfully provided, and featured a stripper, initially dressed in black underwear, pole dancing.

En route to Cát Bà Island we saw isolated floating villages, clusters of colourful wooden houses perched on the water with dogs running the length of the jetty, barking at the boats, and then stopped at Trinh Nũ, a cave of stalactites and stalagmites gouged into a cliff. Like every other remote and isolated location in Asia, there was also a place to buy overpriced Coca-Cola, snack food and Tiger beer.

From the interior of the cave, we could peer out at the World Heritage-listed bay and marvel at its beauty. On closer inspection, we could also marvel as paint, oil and muddy liquid poured into the green water from pipes in the rock wall, and watch rubbish from the tourist boats and floating villages bobbing grossly in the darkened water. Like the man urinating into the sea in Nha Trang, even the most pristine environment in Vietnam seemed to be treated like a toilet.

'What's that?' I asked Rachell, pointing at a white puffy object floating in the water.

'It looks like a plastic bag,' she said, and then it tilted slightly in the tide of water and we saw that the object ebbing and rolling on the surface was a dirty disposable nappy. The upside, I suppose, is that a baby wasn't wearing it at the time.

There was an encore screening of the pole-dancing video when we returned to the boat, but none of us was keen to view it because we already knew how it ended. Eventually we arrived at Cát Bà Island, a place renowned for its natural beauty and biodiversity, and stayed in the small town of Cát Bà for a night.

Sadly, the only things I really recall about Cát Bà are the staggeringly long hair I found in the bok choy at dinner, and the shower tiles in the hotel bathroom, which featured a wall-sized picture of a nude Asian woman, complete with 1970s-style pubic hair, who looked off into the distance, aloof and bored, as you showered in front of her.

The return boat ride from Cát Bà through Ha Long Bay felt like *Groundhog Day*, except all the sights were visited in reverse order: the same beautiful green water, the same stripper taking her clothes off on screen, the same feeling of, 'Are we there yet?' I clearly lacked the attention span required to enjoy cruising on a boat for more than fifteen minutes, but at least the boat hadn't sunk.

After disembarking at the harbour, an adrenaline-fuelled bus ride back to Hanoi was the perfect antidote to a quiet sailing trip. We had one last drunken night in Vietnam before our flight home and although we had only been away for two weeks, it felt like two weeks in dog years.

★

We got to Hanoi airport and prepared to board our flight home, our bags full of trinkets and our carry-on luggage bulging with Weasel coffee paraphernalia. Our haul was tame compared to the Vietnamese man in front of us who had a Samurai sword. He unsheathed it, intending to put it through the metal detector, and we watched as hard-faced policemen escorted him away from the security checkpoint, disappearing him through a side door.

We were returning to flushing toilets and airconditioning, to a city where nobody would be squatting in the street chopping up animal carcasses with a cleaver or selling raw meat that was left out in the sun dripping blood and attracting flies. And, hopefully, Dire Straits wouldn't be playing everywhere we went. Exchanging wild for mild, the reverse culture shock would be almost as jarring.

After the chaos and colour of Vietnam, Australia seemed sterile, quiet and about as exciting as being on a boat, but the bathrooms were truly a joy to behold. There are many things that I take for granted and none more so than the freedom to place waste toilet paper in the toilet after use and flush it to kingdom come. How plumbing works is a mystery to me, a dirty, disgusting mystery, but I didn't consider it a luxury or appreciate the abundance of Western-style toilets and adequate sewerage systems in my life until they weren't around anymore. Like your appendix or the dentist, you don't tend to think of it unless you're forced to.

I was squeamish and sought out non-squat toilets throughout Vietnam like a pig sniffing for truffles, but even if I found one, I couldn't flush anything down it or the sewerage system would collapse. Thus there was a bin, or a plastic bag, or nothing at all, by the side of the toilet for disposal of used paper, which unsurprisingly made the entire bathroom stink like shit, or worse.

Smell is a powerful, transporting sense. A certain moisturiser makes my mum feel close and the smell of paper in bookstores makes me happy. It's been years since this trip to Vietnam, but the smell of defective plumbing, gross as it is, always makes me nostalgic, instantly taking me back to a fun, uncomplicated time with my best friends, before marriages, mortgages and kids, when we travelled through Vietnam together. And while a blocked drain stinks, to be sure, to me it also smells like adventure.

5 The Puffins Have Flown Away For The Winter

After my trip to Vietnam, I had an itch. Fortunately it was just an itch to travel more and not a consequence of scabies, bedbugs or bird flu. Two weeks in Vietnam had been long enough to make being back at home seem like a novelty, and short enough to make me want to leave again as soon as possible. I had forgotten how satisfying it felt to get away from the familiar, and especially from my job, even if the destination offered unique olfactory challenges. But then the hospital didn't always smell so fresh either.

It was my second year working in an oncology ward and looking after very sick patients who were undergoing bone marrow transplants and other gruelling treatments. It wasn't an easy place to work, but for the first time in my life I cared about my job. It was hard not to when you saw the same patients week after week and got to know them and their families on such a personal level. I was there when they arrived, and I was there when they left, *if* they left. Some patients stayed and stayed and didn't get the chance to return home, or even to die in their own bed, because their bodies just couldn't keep up with their disease and they faded under our watch.

Working in that environment made me think about mortality a lot, and how unfair it was that some people couldn't stay alive, no matter how desperately they wanted to be there for their young children, their partner or their eighteenth birthday, while other people didn't care if they lived or died – the way I had felt at my lowest ebb. Life can be very cruel.

Nobody really likes to dwell on the fact that from the moment we're born we're all living on borrowed time and that some of us are going to run out of it faster than others. Yet you could be forgiven for thinking that people do live forever. Most of us take our sweet time and put off until tomorrow, or the next decade, or our entire lives, things that we think we have all the time in the world for. We act as if there's no urgency and no reason to rush, and maybe we *will* have plenty of time, and an able body at our disposal, but maybe we won't. Nobody plans to have a stroke, or a car accident; and cancer, unfortunately, doesn't care that you've been saving up all the good times for when you retire, or that you're deferring one thing or another until it's the 'right' time.

I want everything yesterday, or sooner, and while patience is not something I've been blessed with, fear is something I have in droves. I'm afraid that I'll run out of days before I get to see all the places I want to see and do all of the things I want to do, that I'll get sick and lose my freedom, that I'll miss out. I've always been in a hurry, which may seem like a contradiction since I'm writing this in my pyjamas at two in the afternoon, but the world is a very big place and I don't know how long I have.

Working with patients who had a poor prognosis was predictably depressing and confronting, but it was also inspiring. It reminded me of the things that are important in life, my health, my relationships and seizing the day so that when all is said and done, I'm not left with a steaming pile of regret. Anything else is noise.

I have always preferred to regret the things I've done, rather than regret those I haven't, which means that over the years I have amassed a fairly mortifying catalogue of embarrassments, as well as a history of credit card debt, because I've never let anything as coarse as money or as restrictive as common sense get in my way. Time is, indeed, of the essence, but I may have interpreted that phrase a little too loosely in the past – an awareness of death doesn't automatically give you carte blanche to max out your credit card on a holiday. There's probably a happy medium between being proactive and making a hash of your finances while you follow your heart, but moderation has never really been my strong suit. I tend to hover at one end of the scale or the other.

My great-grandmother had spent more than six weeks on a ship to get to Australia in 1920, the only significant period of travel she experienced in her lifetime, while it had taken me a day to fly to London on my first trip in 1999. Overseas travel was out of bounds for my parents, too, even before we were born, because it had always been prohibitively expensive. Of course, the arrival of three children who expertly drained their resources meant domestic flights, let alone international travel, were out of the question. Most of our family holidays were spent in the car, covering wide expanses of the country. But things had changed. The price of air travel had plummeted over the last thirty years and I didn't even have to leave the house to buy a ticket, I only had to turn on my computer and pick one.

Nothing was more exciting to me than the promise of an overseas holiday, and much like the giddy realisation that as an adult I *could* stock my fridge with nothing but cheese and chocolate if I wanted to because *I was the boss now*, it occurred to me that I could also buy myself a round-the-world ticket if I felt like it. A financial institution that didn't know any better, and obviously didn't know what I was like *at all*, had recently given me a credit card and it was burning a hole in my pocket. I paid scant attention to my finances as a rule, so what was stopping me from making them worse? Self-restraint? I didn't have any.

Around this time you would have heard me saying things like, 'It's only money! Who cares? I could get hit by a truck tomorrow!' I saw people dying at work at regular intervals and money was about as important to them as a hairnet to a bald guy. But if you're going to throw money around like there's no tomorrow, then you'd better hope that there isn't one because if it arrives things are going to get ugly. And if you *do* rack up a bunch of debt, you can bet that you'll be the one who, far from being hit by a truck, lives to be 106.

I paid for the flight with my credit card, and had every intention of repaying the debt before any interest could accumulate, which of course would only happen in my dreams. With the six weeks of annual leave I had saved up taken in one hit, I was going to visit the cities that I most wanted to see: Tokyo, Reykjavik and New York City, with a pit stop somewhere near the middle to visit my sister and my friends in London. It was almost comical that I had zeroed in on some of the world's most expensive cities considering that I was the least equipped to contend with them. It was a match made in accounting hell.

I worked for six months, taking as many extra shifts as I could to bolster my savings, and in August 2006 I was off again. After finishing night shift at the hospital, I went straight to the airport to check in for my flight to Tokyo. By the time I finally boarded, I was having trouble keeping my eyes open. Snug in my window seat with my seatbelt fastened, I put my earplugs in, my eye mask on and fell asleep with my pillow jammed up against the window, and my face jammed into the pillow. I missed every safety announcement, snack, meal and beverage.

When I woke up, I was in Japan, and soon making my way through an airport arrivals area packed with hordes of giggling, hyperventilating schoolgirls who had turned up to see Keanu Reeves (his flight had landed right before mine). It felt like an auspicious start to my holiday, like being shat on by a bird.

Accommodation in Tokyo was expensive, and the Australian dollar wasn't exactly setting the world on fire, so I stayed at a hostel in Asakusa, an older part of the city that is the last stop on the Ginza subway line and had been the major 'entertainment district' of Tokyo until it was blown to smithereens in the Second World War. My hostel was an unimpressive, drab building that boasted 'we are 24 hrs reception' and a 'specious lounge', which was far more accurate than its intended meaning. Nothing was spacious in Tokyo, and especially not my hostel.

My single room was furnished with a bunk bed, and an arm's length of space between it and the wall, but it was expansive compared with the toilet, which was so small and cramped that you had to clamber up on to the toilet seat so you could shut the door, and your knees touched the wall when you sat down. The shower, while clean, was a makeshift construction, with a showerhead emerging from the wall and positioned above the cistern of a disused toilet. The toilet itself was still in place but sealed shut with black plastic and gaffer tape, removing the temptation to multi-task while washing your hair. On the plus side, there was a place to rest your toiletries – on the toilet – and you could sit down if you wanted to shave your legs. The minus was that I was showering in a toilet – even though it wasn't operational, it felt weird. If you put a mattress in your kitchen, stopped cooking food there and called it your bedroom, you'd still be sleeping in the kitchen.

My room was the furthest from the street on the second floor with a window looking out over the Sumida River, providing a view of the Asahi brewery buildings across the water. The Asahi Beer Hall, a black building designed by the French architect and designer Phillippe Starck, was adorned with a large gold sculpture called the Asahi Flame, said to represent the burning heart and frothy head of Asahi Beer. To most people with eyes, though, it resembled a giant golden turd – the reason it was often referred to as *unko-biru* (poo building). Without a doubt, it was the biggest piece of shit I'd ever seen.

Being in Tokyo felt like being on another planet, and it was the cleanest planet in the known universe. Where Vietnam had been dirty and chaotic, Tokyo was neat and tidy with an atmosphere of polite order, unless you were foolish enough to take the subway during peak hour, when every carriage turned into a clown car. The number of people pressed inside defied all reason. I felt I understood the plight of a sandwich filling on a deeper, much more intimate level after making that mistake at Shinjuku station, the busiest train station in Tokyo, *and the world*.

A week in Tokyo was as fascinating as I had hoped it would be, but it was the subtle differences that I noticed more than the obvious contrasts, like the vending machines on the street that sold cigarettes and beer and the respectful silence on public transport when phones were switched to 'Manner Mode' in consideration of fellow passengers. I wasn't used to being on a train without hearing the minutiae of a teenager's relationship angst or a sinewy man with tattooed legs calling somebody a cunt for not giving him a cigarette earlier on the platform.

The pervasive Japanese culture of cute (*kawaii*) meant that if something could be turned into a cute cartoon, it was, and apparently everything could. Even the door of the subway had a cartoon of a yellow cat with a shocked expression and a crumpled tail as a warning not to get caught in the door. Anywhere else, such a sign would have been a dry, informative image of a hand or foot caught in a door with a red circle and a line through the middle (though I'd prefer a decapitated stick figure with the tagline, 'Don't even *think* about suing us. Your untimely death is on you.').

I expected Tokyo to be overflowing with neon signs, sushi and impeccably groomed Japanese people, and it was, but there was one thing I discovered that exceeded all my expectations – the Toto Washlet. This tricked-out loo made every other toilet look like a hole in the ground. I had no idea how important a heated toilet seat, or 'Warmlet', was to me until I sat on one. It felt like my ass had spent a lifetime flying in economy and suddenly found itself upgraded to first class. Like French fries topped with truffle sprinkles or chocolate dipped in chocolate, the Washlet went above and beyond the call of duty and transformed 'going to the toilet' into an *experience*. A control panel offered a range of options, including the ability to play music or the sound of ocean waves to drown out any of the primordial noises being produced. There was a bidet with adjustable water pressure and temperature, a dryer that fanned your bits with warm air and a built-in deodorising system so that everyone could pretend that nothing had happened in the first place. If cleanliness is next to godliness, then my backside was a goddess in Tokyo and I had a new aspiration in life – to possess a Toto of my very own. When that day arrives, and I swear to my ass that it will, I'll know that I've really made something of my life, and that even the depressing, dark moments were worth it, because I got there in the end.

The only downside to my time in Tokyo was on the morning of my departure, when I endeavoured to find my way back to Narita airport by an alternative train route. I thought it would be more direct, but it was only a more direct route to a panic attack because I ended up getting horribly lost, confusing one subway line for another. I was already running late for check-in when the train I was on broke down. The loudspeaker announcement considerately advised passengers of the situation in Japanese, but all I heard was, '*BLAH BLAH BLAH NARITA BLAH BLAH BLAH.*' I didn't know if I should get on the next train, or not, so I decided to follow the lead of a Japanese man who was carrying a suitcase. He didn't board the next train, or the next one, and my nerves were about to snap. Missing my flight from Tokyo to London would also mean missing my connecting flight from London to Reykjavik, and that would mean I would break the world record in ugly crying, currently held by Claire Danes, which would just make her cry more.

My human GPS got on the third train and I followed, hoping desperately that he was going to the airport and not to his aunt's house in Yokohama for the weekend. Fortunately he was going to the airport, and I arrived at the correct terminal right before check-in was about to close. And just when I thought I could relax, I walked around the corner and saw the enormous customs line that I was at the very end of. Sweating and almost in tears, I ran to the front of the line and pointed in a panic at my watch to the Japanese man who was supposed to go next. He kindly let me cut in, possibly because he wanted the sweating, unhinged stranger to get away from him as quickly as possible. If I worked in airport security, I would have pulled me aside for an X-ray because I was so agitated and nervous it looked like I had swallowed thirty heroin balloons.

Passport stamped, I sprinted to the gate and, huffing and puffing, was the last person to take my seat on the plane. The doors closed behind me and we began taxiing out onto the runway, but it took two gin and tonics, a bag of rice crackers and a movie to calm me down.

After a twelve-hour flight, a brief London layover and another three-hour flight, I arrived in Iceland, but the barren, treeless landscape I saw on the bus ride to Reykjavik from the airport made me feel like I had landed on the moon.

I had an agenda for my time in Iceland – I wanted to see a puffin and visit the Blue Lagoon, and anything else was gravy. Puffins are cute but I can't explain my fascination with them any more than I can explain my obsession with lighthouses and old tins. It's just the way I'm built.

Iceland is a volcanically active country, active in the way that a porn star could be described as being sexually active or an Olympian as physically active. Basically, it's a country that smells like a fart. The rotten egg odour of sulphur is overwhelming at first, but it doesn't take long to get used to it, and after a while you don't really notice it anymore, unless you have a shower or wash your hands with hot water and the steamy emissions envelop you with no chance of escape. Anyway, it's not so bad when you know that the smell has emerged from the bowels of the earth rather than the bowels of a human.

The bits of Iceland that aren't fiery volcanoes and hot springs are fairly cold, hence the name, so when I got to my hotel in Reykjavik with a six-pack of duty-free beer, I discovered that my room didn't have a bar fridge, but that I could leave the beer out on the window ledge and the cold weather would perform the same service. Iceland wasn't just cold, though, it was cool. That you were visiting the land of Björk, arguably the country's most famous export, wasn't something you could easily forget because her albums were for sale all over Reykjavik and within arm's reach on most shop counters, even if all you needed was a napkin.

I knew that Iceland was going to be expensive because I had booked a hotel room in Reykjavik for the first two nights of my eight-day stay as a 'special treat' and while it was a fairly modest hotel, the cost was astronomical. However, I wasn't quite prepared for the reality of being in a country that wanted to bleed me dry. In 2006, Reykjavik had a well-deserved spot on the list of the world's most expensive cities, in the top five, no less, so I had *no* business being in such a place, or at the restaurant I had chosen for dinner as another 'special treat', the justification I use for doing whatever I want at least once. I paid with my credit card, as usual, and when I got back to the hotel I worked out how much dinner had cost in Australian dollars, and discovered that I had just eaten a week's rent. I decided that I would see as much of Iceland as I could in the time that I was there, because I would have to find myself a wealthy dying relative or a pimp if I ever wanted to come back.

The first order of business was seeing a puffin, so I walked down to the Old Harbour feeling more excited than a kid who's been 'good' and thinks the obese gentleman in the red suit is going to make it rain toys in the morning. I knew the 'Puffin Express' sightseeing tour left from the harbour every two hours during the day. The only problem was that it left every two hours during the day from May until August, and I had arrived in the middle of September. The solitary puffin I found at the harbour was drawn on a sign that said, 'Sorry! The puffins have flown away for the winter!'

Those adorable, feathery *assholes*! If I could make it all the way to Iceland from Australia to see them, surely they could have delayed their winter holiday by a couple of days, but no. Apparently it was imperative that the puffins reside at their southern beach home before they caught a chill. I was disappointed, to put it mildly, and angry with myself for not being more diligent in my research. I had flown to Iceland expecting to see a puffin on demand, like a tourist standing outside the Opera House in the middle of Sydney asking where the kangaroos were. Yes, I was *that* moron.

I did see a puffin later that day – in fine slices on a sashimi plate with its friends the Icelandic horse and the minke whale. I had a salad, instead, and a new definition of heartbreak.

Besides puffins, there were plenty of other impressive attractions in Iceland, like glaciers and geysers and waterfalls. The trick was working out how to *get* to them. I didn't have a driver's licence at the time, and although hiring a car probably would have cost me more than the deposit on a house, it would have been fun to see the country without having to join a group tour and being restricted to its sights. But that's exactly what happened, and I ended up on a tour with couples from England, France and America, and an Icelandic driver/tour guide called Olaf in … a monster truck.

A monster truck looks ridiculous, and riding in one made me feel ridiculous, but it was great being able to drive through a river to get to a glacier, which almost made up for the fact that I felt like I needed a spinal realignment afterwards. Travelling solo is usually something I enjoy, because I have the freedom to do whatever I want whenever I want, but being the only single person in a group of couples was not as pleasant as it could have been. It wasn't the 'being alone' part that bothered me, or even the personalities of the other couples – they were all perfectly nice people. My beef was with Olaf, who wouldn't leave me alone and couldn't take a hint. Every time we stopped, he would try to cajole me into sitting in the front seat next to him.

'I get car sick in the front seat,' I lied.

'I have bag,' he said, undeterred, 'for sick.'

Fortunately, the American gentleman, a lovely fellow from Ohio, came to my rescue.

'Well, I *love* being in the front! I'll be your wingman, Olaf!' he said, winking at me. Olaf looked unimpressed and slightly confused. I don't think he knew what a wingman was, but a middle-aged man certainly wasn't his idea of one.

The scenery of Iceland was dramatic. Much of the land was flat and unremarkable, and just when you thought there was nothing to see, you would arrive at a thunderous waterfall or a stunning crater lake with luminous green water. The earth was alive: steam rose from the ground in the distance and sporadic bursts of boiling water erupted violently into the air, reminding me of the overwhelming power of nature and my place as a speck in the grand scheme of things.

The tour went well, Olaf's persistent advances aside. At one stage I thought I'd found the perfect way to avoid conversation with him by listening to music on my iPod, but he simply took one ear bud from my ear and said, 'What are we listening to?' before sticking it into his own hole.

On the way back to Reykjavik we had to stop at a garage to replace a flat tyre, which is not such a big deal if you're in a car but is a much bigger deal, literally, if you're in a monster truck. The garage had a diner, where we had cups of coffee while we waited for the tyre to be fixed, and with red and white checked cloths on the table we could have been at a diner by a highway in America, except for the availability of fermented fish snacks and the fact that a coffee cost ten dollars.

Eventually we were on the road again, and the English couple asked Olaf about the Northern Lights, and how likely it would be for us to see them at this time of year.

'Maybe, maybe not.' He shrugged. 'I can do night tour for you tonight?'

The couples began to discuss whether they wanted to go out again when it got dark.

Olaf looked at me in the rear-view mirror. 'You want to see the Northern Lights?' he asked, which may or may not have been code for his genitals. I politely declined.

Olaf began dropping everyone back to their respective hotels, and when I realised he had put mine last on the schedule and I was in imminent danger of being left alone with him I jumped out when the Americans did. I thanked him and mumbled something about going to church.

I did my own Northern Lights tour that night, walking down by the waterfront when it was dark, and I either saw the faintest green glow in the sky, or was hallucinating – maybe I was just happy to be alone.

I wasn't happily alone for long. Unable to maintain the hotel accommodation to which I would love to have become accustomed, I moved to a hostel that was less crippling financially, but still very expensive. Slightly less insanely priced accommodation was a magnet for everybody in Reykjavik who wasn't an heir or heiress, so the hostel was busy, loud, and full of kids on a school camp, which meant that it was like trying to fall asleep at a sold-out Justin Bieber concert.

I remembered the camps of my school days, and how removing teenagers from their homes for several days seemed to be an invitation to unleash mayhem. Sugar-fuelled and sleep-deprived, we invariably went on the rampage, blasting each other with shaving cream missiles and flour bombs and orchestrating elaborate stunts like moving all the furniture out of a room and stacking it in a towering pile in a bathroom. It was great fun, and the fun didn't stop until the camp was over and everybody, especially the exhausted teachers, went home to rest and recover. Well, what goes around comes around. My tomfoolery at school camps came back at me tenfold at the hostel as a bunch of Spanish teenagers ran up and down the hallways, screaming and laughing all night after apparently having slipped their supervising teachers Rohypnol. I stood at the doorway of my room in my pyjamas, swearing and glaring at them to no avail, with hair like a messy, tangled hat.

When I left Iceland, I spent a week in London with my sister, Jo (the second Chambers child to utilise the British

Working Holiday visa), her boyfriend, Tony, and my friends who still lived in the city. Although my sister would never forget or forgive me for laughing when a cupboard fell on her as a small child (a response I maintain stemmed from shock and not malice) we were very close. She was three years younger than me but people usually assumed that she was the older sister because she was inherently more mature and level-headed. She was twelve and doing her homework at the kitchen table when I'd emerged from my bedroom as a fifteen-year-old, crying hysterically, to call an ambulance after I'd taken the overdose. I remember her shouting at me, 'What have you done?' before calling my mother at work and coolly telling her to come home because there was an emergency. I'm not sure if it was then, or in the years afterwards when I was clearly unwell, but a dynamic developed where she became my protector, and even though I was supposed to be the older sister, it didn't feel like I was. It still doesn't. Along with my parents and younger brother, she is more aware of my vulnerability than anyone.

Like sisters of any age, a history of fighting like snarling cats and rabid dogs had given way to a less fractious relationship as we grew older, which was aided by distance (with each of us living in England for an extended period) and destroyed by its removal. After a few days of my presence in her shared house, Jo told me that she had really looked forward to my arrival in London, but she was even more excited about my imminent departure.

Ah, *sisters*.

*

I was on my way to the airport for the last leg of my trip, New York City, where my boyfriend at the time, Greg, was going to meet up with me. After a month being a law unto myself, having to consider somebody else's wishes was not going to come naturally.

Much as I hadn't read up on puffin season in Reykjavik, I hadn't checked my flight time before booking a taxi to the airport so I arrived at Heathrow at five in the morning under the impression, for some reason, that I had an 8 a.m. flight. As the airline employee informed me when I went to check in, my flight wasn't until three in the afternoon. I really needed to start *reading things* and stop looking at the pictures.

Fortunately, there was a seat available on an earlier flight, and since I was going to be spending time waiting at an airport either way, I decided to take it. I imagined that there would be a lounge at JFK International Airport where I could kick back and relax, perhaps sipping a martini, while I waited for my travel companion to arrive from Australia. Clearly, I thought I was flying back to the 1960s or into an episode of *Mad Men*.

The airport terminal turned out to have a *Hudson News* stand, a kiosk that sold dry muffins as big as bowling balls and a row of uncomfortable plastic chairs that didn't stand up well to eight hours of sitting. And it all went downhill from there.

When you travel with someone, you'll inevitably be tested, individually and as a couple, and if you realise after two days in the same space that you've already failed the test, then you have discovered a way to make a relatively short holiday feel like a six-month tour of duty. Well done.

Before I ever went to New York City, I had a picture in my mind of what it would be like, and that picture was the bastard child of *Crocodile Dundee* and *Sex and the City*. New York was where Woody Allen and Soon-Yi and Sarah Jessica Parker lived, where jogging was a potential threat to your personal safety and being mugged or shot was par for the course. I knew that I should hand all my money to the first menacing stranger who accosted me to prevent being gunned down in the street like Patrick Swayze in *Ghost*. But beyond the wall-to-wall danger (and more importantly to me), New York City was the home of the bagel, my doughy spirit animal.

The city I met face to face in 2006 bore little resemblance to the one my imagination had conjured up by pureeing pop culture and current affairs into a glittery, topical paste. I didn't feel unsafe, even with the disappeared Twin Towers, now a busy construction site and a terrible reminder of the cruelty that can lie in wait, and I didn't go jogging in Central Park (or anywhere else for that matter), but I walked through it several times, stalking squirrels, which were exotic to me, and took photographs without injury.

The most frightening thing I saw in New York was the scores of women walking around Manhattan with hairlines that began on top of their skulls and eyes that stretched all the way to their ears. The overall effect wasn't one of prolonged youthfulness, as hoped, but an uneven, discordant ghoulishness that made me sad. What did these women see when they looked in the mirror, their faces stripped of softness and character? Being able to afford as much plastic surgery as you wanted seemed a lot more dangerous than travelling on the subway.

Relationship-wise, the shit hit the fan fairly early on, when Greg flippantly described a bagel as 'just a bread roll with a hole in the middle' on the third day and I reacted as though he had kicked a puppy into orbit. Clearly, we were horribly ill-suited and our relationship had no future, but there were still ten days and a twenty-two-hour flight before we could officially go our separate ways, so we did our best to tolerate each other's company. 'Tolerating each other's company' meant that we avoided each other during the day under the guise of pursuing different interests within a limited time-frame, and only saw each other at night if we ate dinner together. It went unspoken by us both, but the inevitable break-up conversation, along with the financial consequences of my holiday, could wait until we were back in Australia. In the meantime there was music to buy and film production assistants to upset.

One afternoon I was looking for a record store in Noho, the part of the city north of Houston Street, when I noticed some of the roads were cordoned off, and a caravan of rental trucks were parked nearby. I found the store along a dusty, deserted street lined with what looked like abandoned cars and tumbleweeds. Nobody said anything when I walked into the street and into the store, but when I wanted to leave, a bossy man wearing a headset put his arm up to block the door and said bluntly, 'You can't leave, we're filming. I'll let you know when you can go.'

'Oh, okay,' I said, and I waited for five minutes with a couple of other grumbling people who acted like they had very important shit to do and places to be. I didn't, but I didn't like being told what to do or where I could and couldn't go. Last time I checked, it was a free country. Isn't that what America was *all about*?

'What are they filming anyway?' one guy asked the human barricade.

'New Will Smith film,' he replied.

The guy rolled his eyes. 'Great,' he said sarcastically. *'Another* Will Smith movie. Just what the world needs.'

'Okay, you can go now, but hurry!' the headset guy with the bloated sense of importance said impatiently. I walked out and headed north while the other people went south. I had only taken a few steps when a man across the street started screaming, 'YOU'RE IN THE SHOT! GET OUTTA THE SHOT! *RUN!*'

Asking me to run was a waste of the very loud man's time, and I didn't care for his tone, either, so I continued walking down the street with great dignity.

A year or two later, when I saw *I Am Legend*, a movie with the tagline 'THE LAST MAN ON EARTH IS NOT ALONE', I figured they were referring to me, walking down the street with my bag of records.

Despite the awkward personal situation, being in New York was exciting. I spent a lot of time walking along the streets and avenues that I knew from so many movies and television shows and books. I was in the city of Andy Warhol's Factory and J.D. Salinger's *The Catcher in the Rye*. I stood on the street outside Truman Capote's house in Brooklyn Heights. It was pop culture heaven. On the last day I saw a dog wearing a raincoat, the *Ghostbusters* firehouse in Tribeca and was underwhelmed by a Magnolia Bakery cupcake. I remember standing on Fifth Avenue, observing the crazy snarled traffic and listening to the noise, and thinking, 'I wish I could live here.'

It was a potent wish, as it turned out, and if I'd known the universe was listening, I would have added, 'and had a million dollars.'

I flew out of New York with my soon to be ex-boyfriend, determined to return again one day under different circumstances, but first I had to face the music.

6   Fanny Ice Cream

The last part of a holiday, the bit where you've run out of money and you're travelling back home with a bag of dirty washing and a bottomless pit of dread in your stomach, only to be greeted by a pile of bills, a dead plant and an empty fridge, practically undoes all the good work of going on holiday in the first place. Nothing beats the natural high of leaving to explore other regions of the world, and nothing is quite as depressing as coming back down to earth with an audible thud as you're forced to face reality. Clinical depression is similar to that post-holiday let-down; the only difference is that it sticks around instead of fading within a week or two as you fall back into your usual routine.

There's a certain anxiety I feel after an extreme haircut where I don't recognise the person staring back at me in the mirror (I call it 'hair trauma™'). Returning home after a long holiday gives me the same feeling about my life. After six weeks of setting my own schedule and doing as I pleased in various locations around the globe, snapping back to my regular existence felt like whiplash. It was a shock to the system that took some time to adjust to: it wasn't just that I was back at work paying for the financial damage I had done on holiday, or that Greg and I had promptly broken up. The break-up itself was fairly bloodless, given that we had only been together for a few months and by the end we didn't even like each other that much, but I would still have preferred to be poked in the eye with a stick. On top of that, I was also at the furthest point from the next holiday.

Destroying a credit card is a lot of fun, but soon enough, it's the credit card's turn to destroy you and that part is a lot less enjoyable and lasts significantly longer, much like the nine-month gestation period of a baby compared with the fifteen minutes spent creating it. I had some serious cleaning up to do, and working permanent night shift at the hospital was the most expedient way to shrink my debt, though it also shrank my feelings of happiness and my tolerance for just about everything else. Since passing out from exhaustion during the day doesn't have the same calming, restorative effect as sleeping at night (the way the human body is designed to), my fairly short fuse became even shorter and if I woke up to find there was no milk in the fridge, or we had run out of coffee, then *someone* was going to be *sorry they were ever born* as I stormed around the house looking for a shadow to punch. I really wasn't my 'best self' on night shift.

The oncology ward I worked on was usually crazy-busy, even at night, with medications and blood products administered around the clock, but at the odd times it *was* quiet, one of my favourite things to do was to look up flights online and plan my next travel itinerary. Doing so had beneficial properties. Anything that reminded me why I was staying awake all night, and why I went to work at all, was a good thing because whenever fatigue descended, as it inevitably did at three in the morning, I had a morbid existential crisis. Finessing prospective travel plans gave me a sense of purpose and a reason to get out of bed, even if it wasn't until late in the afternoon. A career in nursing offered many valuable things in addition to money, but my life still felt directionless and travel gave it structure, or at least something to aim for. A lot of the other nurses I worked with had children and mortgages, which are also valid reasons to avoid unemployment, but I felt detached from their world. I didn't have a mortgage or a car because they were anchors, responsibilities, which would tie me down. Just the thought of them made me feel anxious and claustrophobic. I had an issue with commitment, I couldn't even handle a dog, and where others had a maternal instinct, I seemed to only have wanderlust and pet envy.

It took four months to move my financial circumstance from dire to less dire, and my romantic life was looking up, too – a long-term friendship had turned into a relationship. Things were going well with my old pal/new boyfriend, Dave, and I gave myself something new to look forward to by buying another ticket to Asia. I wasn't yet out of the woods financially, but I needed a goal to keep my boat afloat because without one, my natural tendency was to sink like a stone. Knowing that excitement and stimulation was on the horizon helped me to keep the bigger picture in focus, because apparently being able to pay for my own food, shelter and utilities wasn't a satisfying enough outcome for me. I needed a little glitter on top.

After the ridiculous expense of my round-the-world holiday, returning to Asia was particularly appealing because it wasn't going to cost me an arm and a leg, unless, of course, I was mowed down by traffic. There was a much higher probability of that occurring than I cared to dwell on but it wasn't going to keep me at home.

I was working a stretch of nights with my friends Renee and Eileen, and it seemed the travel bug I'd caught was contagious because by the end of the week, the three of us had arranged time off, bought our tickets and were busily compiling lists of things to see. Eileen was a senior nurse on the ward so she could only arrange two weeks off, but Renee and I had started as new graduates together just two years earlier and our comparative lack of experience worked to our advantage in this instance. We were able to negotiate a six-week absence and it was unlikely anybody would even notice we were gone.

The next two months at work took on a new shine as I counted down the days until we were on our way to the airport and heading to my favourite part – the area marked 'Departures'.

Vietnam had been so memorable that I was keen to go back and explore the parts of the country I hadn't seen, and see more of the places I had, and since neither Eileen nor Renee had been to Asia before, I was the default tour leader – a position I felt ill-equipped to handle. (I like to play the tough guy, but if you push me, I'm going to fall over.)

Unlike my first trip to Vietnam, when I had flown to Ho Chi Minh City in the south and out of Hanoi in the north, this one began in Hanoi. After some half-hearted negotiation, we took a taxi from the airport into the city, a car ride I *thought* I was prepared for. I took the front seat, while Eileen and Renee, innocent lambs to the slaughter, sat in the back with all our bags. If they were anything like me, their first impressions of Vietnam's traffic chaos would be slightly scarring. Driving in Vietnam was not for the faint-hearted.

As we left the airport and turned on to a busier road, we were tailing a flat-tray truck carrying piles of stacked bricks. It became apparent after a short distance, when the truck's speed began to increase, that the bricks weren't actually secured in any way because they began falling off the open tray and hurtling down the road towards us. The taxi driver yelled, trying to dodge the debris while doing his best not to turn into oncoming traffic, but some contact was unavoidable and several bricks bounced up and under the car with frighteningly loud bangs. Eileen and Renee screamed, and I stared in horror, shielding my head with my arms when it looked like a brick-missile was going to launch through the windscreen and rearrange my face. Finally the truck took a left turn, showering the road with even more bricks as it veered. There wasn't going to be anything left on the back when it got to wherever it was going. The imminent threat removed, I turned to check on the others in the back seat.

'You guys okay?' I asked, but they were obviously not okay. They were wide-eyed with fear and cowering behind their backpacks.

'No.' Eileen shook her head.

'I want to go home,' Renee said.

'Welcome to Vietnam!' I said, and my ever-reliable reaction to shock, nervous laughter, kicked in and it took quite a while for me to stop.

The steel rod travellers need in their spines to avoid being fleeced was evidently missing from mine, which is how we ended up staying in the hotel chosen by our taxi driver instead of the one we'd planned to stay in. In my defence, my brain was still too numb with fear after the brick incident to present a coherent opposition. He could have sold me a rainbow at that point and I would have told him to keep the change.

Our room was on the fourth floor of a house, and it was clean, if not a little threadbare. It could have been a lot worse, and all we really cared about by then was taking a shower because we'd broken a sweat climbing the stairs with our backpacks. Although we were used to humidity living in Brisbane's tropical climate, this was a new level of soup-like saturation.

'Where's the airconditioner?' Renee asked as she fanned herself with a magazine. I looked around the room, behind the thin curtains, in the cupboards, and even checked the bathroom before admitting defeat.

'There isn't one.'

'Oh, god,' Eileen said.

There was a ceiling fan, however, so we opened the window to let in a breeze, and turned the fan to the highest setting. Within twenty seconds it began to smoke and our room smelt strongly of burning electrical wire, the sort of acrid stink that infiltrates your clothes, hair and skin for days afterwards. I turned it off before it caught fire, exploded or flew off and decapitated us all.

Our accommodation stank, but now that the adrenaline crash was kicking in after the brick incident, none of us had the energy to look for another place. A similar thing happens after medical emergencies at the hospital. Adrenaline levels surging, we can spend half an hour or more furiously trying to resuscitate a dying patient and whether we are successful in our efforts or not, *we* are dead on our feet within the hour. The energy slump after the crisis leaves us feeling unimaginably tired.

Cyclos, awning-covered three-wheeled bicycles with a scooped seat at the front for a passenger, became our newest terrifying mode of transport. The cyclo driver madly pedalling behind had the passenger as a barrier, but there was nothing between the passenger and oncoming traffic except for luck and skin. After surviving a fraught trip to and from the Temple of Literature, one of Hanoi's impressive ancient landmarks, we stopped for a cool treat at the amusingly named 'Fanny Ice Cream'. I took pictures of the sign and snickered. Sometimes I wonder if I'm Peter Pan's long-lost immature sister and that I'm never going to grow up. I know that sort of thing *should* get old at some point, but it hasn't yet and maybe it never will.

From Hanoi, Renee, Eileen and I took an overnight train to Sapa, a beautiful, mountainous region close to China. We had arranged a two-day hiking trip of the area in advance, something I can only blame on a contact high from breathing in exhaust fumes in Hanoi and my failure to pay attention to the 'mountainous' part in the fine print.

There is nothing about me that says 'hiker': not my shoes, not my complexion and certainly not my physical fitness and, while I've always been a big fan of walking (it's my only consistent form of exercise), hiking and the outdoors in general do not agree with my constitution and I hate their guts. How do I know they don't agree with me? Well, if it's hot, my face will be red and if it's really cold, my face will be red, and if I have exerted myself physically in any way, my face will be red. And if I've just walked up a mountain in Vietnam in the summertime, my face will be purple and swear words will be pouring out of my mouth. It's not very becoming.

While Eileen, Renee and I were walking *down*hill, I had surprised myself by enjoying hiking immensely. The views of the surrounding mountains and terraced rice fields were spectacular and it was lovely to be out in the country and breathing fresh air after days spent in bustling, manic Hanoi. But when we had walked all the way to the bottom and had to begin walking back up, I didn't love it quite so much. Motorbike taxis circled the base of the mountain, waiting to drive lazy or unfit tourists back up to town, but pride saw me wave them away. How bad could it be? The first incline hadn't been all *that* steep.

There have been many times in my life where I have displayed staggeringly poor judgment, and not accepting a ride back up the mountain was yet another of them. By the time I had realised the error of my ways, I was thirsty, breathless and panting by the side of the road with a face like a beetroot, and there were no motorbikes to be seen because all the intelligent people had taken them. Eileen and Renee may well have resented the hiking as much as I did, but they were a lot quieter about it than me. Eileen played on a netball team and Renee was a regular gym attendee, so I was definitely the odd man out with all my gasping and wheezing.

I would like to think that when the going gets tough I can draw on my inner strength to face adversity with grace and dignity, but the truth is I've never demonstrated any of these qualities in my life. What usually happens in such situations is that I blow a gasket, swear, scream, shout, stamp my feet, kick things and generally act like an outrageous asshole, and I did a few of those things ascending the mountain. Renee and Eileen stopped to watch me, bemused by my outburst, sensibly conserving their energy for the duration of the trek. Tantrum over, I realised that the only alternative was to lie down by the side of the road and remain there until I died, leaving my body to be eaten by wild animals, so I pulled myself together, resumed walking and made it back to Sapa, eventually, where I collapsed in a hideous, sweating heap. And thus day one of the *two-day* hiking excursion was complete.

The second day wasn't much of an improvement. It had rained overnight and when we were dropped off at the starting point in the morning by the hotel minibus, I was handed a walking stick that was more 'tree branch' than sturdy cane and which turned out to be essential from the get-go, as the hike began by descending a muddy slope.

'Everyone, follow me!' ordered our guide, and he darted nimbly down the muddy track as if he were part man, part mountain goat. I hung back and watched as the rest of the group carefully made their way down the hill, successfully using their sticks to maintain their balance in obviously slippery conditions. Then it was my turn. I was the last person standing at the top.

'You can do this,' I told myself. I took one tentative step and immediately slid for three metres in the mud, throwing my arms up in to the air to avoid landing on my face and sending my walking stick flying.

'Fuck it, you can't do this!' corrected my inner voice. I scrambled back up the slope, smearing myself in mud, and transforming my Converse sneakers into what appeared to be clogs made out of clay. I took it as a sign.

'I'll see you later!' I called out to Eileen and Renee, who were already at the bottom of the slope with the rest of the group, waiting for me. 'I'm going back into town.' Renee looked as though she was in two minds about joining me, but she went on with Eileen and I started walking.

A minute later, a man on a motorbike was hovering alongside me, the tinny engine buzzing like a mosquito.

'You nee ride?' he asked me. Of course there was a ride on offer today, when the sun was hiding behind a cloud and the road back was as flat as a fucking pancake.

'No, but thanks,' I told him, and he shrugged and zoomed off, disappearing around the bend.

After Sapa, we returned to Hanoi on the train, and then tried to figure out the best way to get south to Hue and Hoi An since there weren't any train tickets available and the idea of driving out to the airport again didn't thrill the others.

'It's too soon,' Renee said, 'I'm still getting over the ride in.'

'There is overnight bus,' the helpful woman at the travel agency told us. 'Very nice bus with beds, you sleep, *sleep*, wake up in Hue!'

A sleeper bus was the one mode of transport in Vietnam that I hadn't yet tried and it didn't sound that different from the overnight train, although it was cheaper, so we bought our tickets, ate some dinner and waited at the designated bus stop in the dark with our bags, feeling excited about the next part of our journey.

I'm mildly claustrophobic, and it seems to be getting worse as I get older. It's not so bad that I freak out in a lift or an enclosed space, I just hate feeling trapped. Unless I know that I have a way out of wherever I am, even if I'm staying over at a friend's house, my anxiety starts to balloon. Sometimes if I *really* try to relax and breathe deeply I can stop the feeling from becoming overwhelming, but at other times the circumstances are not conducive to finding or maintaining a sense of calm. Travelling on a sleeper bus in Vietnam is one of those circumstances. Calling it a 'sleeper' bus was an outrageous lie but some degree of poetic licence was necessary because nobody would buy a ticket for a 'Terrifying, Cramped, Trying Not to Cry Bus' or 'The Hell on Wheels Experience'.

When the bus pulled up at our stop, it didn't look anything like the pictures the lady at the travel agency had shown us. It looked like a hostel that had had sex with a funeral home, with rows and rows of narrow bunk frames crammed into the available space each holding 'beds' that resembled fibreglass coffins.

'*Shit!*' we said in unison, but this was our ride whether we liked it or not so we climbed aboard. Besides acute disappointment, the next obstacle was finding a coffin to call home for the night because the bus was full. We stood in the aisles with our giant backpacks, knocking into everything and unsure what to do next. The next moment the bus driver began yelling and some Vietnamese passengers vacated their pods so we could have them, which felt creepily intimate, like sitting on a toilet seat that's still warm from the previous occupant, and also made us look and feel like white supremacists.

'They didn't have sleeper tickets,' a man on the top bunk a berth down advised me. 'You didn't steal their seats.'

'Oh, okay,' I said, uneasily, but it still begged the question of where those passengers would go since the bus was now completely full. A few moments later they began to set up camp in the aisle, and my question was answered.

Then more and more people climbed on to the bus until the aisles were completely choked with humans and the bus had become a mobile flophouse, with bottles of liquor being passed up and down.

Renee, Eileen and I had slotted in wherever there was an available space, which meant that we were scattered around the bus like pollen. I was in a pod at floor level in the middle of the bus, effectively lying in a sea of bodies with other people's feet resting beside my head and my claustrophobia already raging. Eileen was further back and off to the side and Renee had basically disappeared into a dark corner, lying on the floor in a row of bodies at the very back. The only available place to store our luggage was *nowhere*, so we hugged our backpacks like security blankets or used them as chunky uncomfortable pillows and jammed our hand luggage down into the base of the coffin around our feet, which further heightened the sense of being entombed. In addition, the apparent absence of a vehicle suspension system created the sensation of having your teeth shaken loose from your skull.

In theory the sleeper bus should have been a pleasant way to travel a long distance, especially compared with sitting upright in economy on a plane, when I'd give just about anything to be able to lie down. But in a plane, even with turbulence and a middle of the aisle seat, you're still floating on air and the drone of the engines creates a consistent wall of sound that makes sleep accessible. On the bus, we felt every bump on the road, which seemed to be made mostly of bumps, as we lay prone, on edge and wide awake with the bus driver's constant swerving and blasting of the horn destroying any chance of sleep. The bus then broke down and we were stuck for two hours on the side of the road beside a stagnant swamp. Interestingly, it wasn't the hellish smell inside and out of the bus that was upsetting me as much as knowing that while the bus was stationary, we weren't getting any closer to our time on it ending. Telling ourselves that it would eventually be over because we would either arrive in Hue or crash into a ditch was the only comfort at hand. Being stuck on the bus *for no reason* made me want to weep, but I'm pretty sure the universe was laughing at me because, historically, whenever I think, 'Okay, this really is the WORST time of my ENTIRE LIFE,' the universe responds with, 'Oh, yeah? *I'll* give you something to cry about, you whiny baby!' Far from falling on deaf ears, my complaints are heard, interpreted as a dare and returned to sender as a lesson in gratitude.

'Perhaps you should have been grateful that you were stuck on this shitty bus when it was MOVING,' the universe says. 'And *maybe* you should be counting your blessings that you don't need to go to the toilet right now … because I could make this much worse for you, you know. Just TRY ME.'

At some stage the bus must have been fixed and I must have fallen asleep, because I woke up from a lovely dream that I wasn't on the bus only to find myself still on the bus and really needing to pee. When we stopped for an early morning 'refreshment' break, there was an unsurprising stampede for the squat toilet. Nobody had standards anymore.

When we finally escaped the bus in Hue, my anxiety began to dissipate and I felt that I knew the true meaning of joy. If we had to cover any significant distance from that point on, we were taking a flight, no matter how many bricks bounced in our direction on the drive to the airport.

I usually have trouble recalling what I ate for breakfast because my short-term memory is terrible, but I am pretty good at remembering directions when I'm travelling. Since I was retracing my steps by returning to Hue and Hoi An, I could recommend hotels and places to eat and where to avoid a massage unless one was feeling particularly bold. The familiarity was soothing; the prospect of being stranded in Hue was not. Shortly after we arrived, so had the teeming rain I also remembered from my first trip, and when the streets around out hotel began flooding, we erred on the side of caution and took the next bus out of town to Hoi An.

Showing Renee and Eileen my photos of Hoi An was what had sold them on a trip to Vietnam in the first place, and they weren't disappointed when they saw it in the flesh. Having learnt from my earlier visit, we didn't spend all our time getting clothes sewn on to our bodies, or buying uncomfortable shoes that smelt overwhelmingly like industrial adhesive. Instead, we hired bikes, rode all over town and shopped. We bought so much brightly coloured lacquer ware, plates, bowls and trays, that each of us had to send a box of our new purchases home. The international postage was a costly exercise, but the alternative, emptying our bags and throwing away all of our clothes, held little appeal.

We spent four days in lovely, relaxing Hoi An before taking another bus to Dalat. It appeared to be a sprawling seaside city, but all I saw of it I spied out of a bus window, en route to the airport.

From Dalat, we flew to Ho Chi Minh City and I felt a strong sense of déjà vu as I stood outside the arrivals area arguing with the taxi drivers. I was a little less green now, and a lot less intimidated by confrontation, so I had no qualms about negotiating a reasonable fare. We eventually reached an agreement with a man who spoke next to no English and who just nodded a lot as he directed us with enthusiastic hand gestures to his car in the middle of the car park. And *what a car it was.*

At one stage it had probably been white, but it was now mostly brown with rust, so much so that the boot of the car was held shut by a length of rope threaded through two large rust holes and tied in a knot. If the exterior was any indication of the car's health, it wasn't a good omen for ours, yet we couldn't fault the pleasantness of our driver, who smiled at us as he untied the rope, then took each of our backpacks and threw them in. Ordinarily, the movement of throwing a bag into a car wouldn't have created any momentum, but in this case, the car started to roll forward because the brakes were obviously as fucked as the parts of the vehicle we *could* see. The driver ran around and jumped into the front seat, pressing hard enough on the pedal to bring the car to a faltering stop.

'Oh my *god*,' I said, starting to giggle, mostly out of fear, because getting in his car was probably going to be the most dangerous thing we would do in Vietnam, but since our bags were now in the back of this beast and the past eleven days had worn down our capacity to exercise caution, we got in anyway. I sat in the front seat, again, while Eileen and Renee sat in the back and we all hoped for the best, but realistically expected the worst.

Surprisingly, the car was operational, although very sluggish, and we managed to leave the airport and enter the fray of traffic. While we were nervous passengers, our driver looked like the happiest man on earth. It was refreshing, at first, for our company to be appreciated, and then it was alarming because he stopped looking at the road and smiled at me instead, with the occasional cursory glance ahead the only indication that he even realised he was behind the wheel of a car on a busy road.

'I think *someone's* got a crush on you,' Eileen commented as she and Renee laughed from the back seat and I squirmed in the front. Unwanted attention is one thing, but when the attention-giver is ultimately responsible for your safety and is paying none to the task of negotiating traffic conditions, that's quite another. The fact that his car could only reach a maximum speed of 50 kilometres an hour may have been our sole protective factor, as it gave the other vehicles on the road a chance to avoid us.

Eventually, miraculously, we ended up at our hotel in the backpackers' hub of the city despite the enamoured driver writing his phone number down on a piece of paper, drawing a little love heart next to it and handing it to me without once looking at the road, much to the amusement of my friends.

'You've still got it,' Renee said, giving me a wink.

'Shut up.'

Ho Chi Minh City was Eileen's last hurrah. She was flying back to Brisbane and returning to work, while Renee and I were continuing on to Cambodia. From there we would head to Laos to meet another nurse friend, Darren, and the three of us would travel through Thailand together. We still had a month of travel ahead of us. It felt great knowing that we still had so much time to wander.

There was a lot to be thankful for when I took stock of our time in Vietnam. None of us had fallen off a mountain in Sapa, or got sick, the sleeper bus nightmare was firmly in the past and would never be repeated, our small plane from Dalat had delivered us unscathed to Ho Chi Minh City and my taxi-driving suitor hadn't killed us en route from the airport. We went to the bar downstairs from our hotel to drink dollar beers and celebrate having made it this far, on the off-chance that the Mekong Delta boat tour we were doing the next day ended with any or all of us drowning, because there was still plenty of time for something to go horribly wrong.

Striking up a conversation with people you meet in bars in Vietnam, or anywhere for that matter, is not always advisable. The prostitutes whose turf you are on may view you as a threat to their livelihood, bombarding you with filthy looks, and sometimes your fellow English speakers are people whose reasons for being in Asia seem sketchy, at best, and whose only form of personal growth is likely to be skin cancer and sexually transmitted diseases. You may have a language in common, but it doesn't mean you understand one another. One Australian gentleman we chatted to advised us that we should try drinking snake blood for its potent aphrodisiac effect, over-sharing with tales of his subsequent raging day-long boner. He also told Renee and me that we *had* to visit a shooting range when we got to Cambodia.

'You can shoot *anything* at those places!' he said, excitedly. 'I mean, really, ANYTHING. They have every sort of weapon you can imagine; handguns, rifles, *hand grenades*. It's out of this world. You can blow up a cow with a fucking *bazooka* if you want to!'

'Why the fuck would anyone want to do that?' I asked him, appalled.

'Just because you *can*! Asia is like the Wild West, you can do anything you want if you have the money,' he said, then lowered his voice: 'I've heard that if you have the cash, you can shoot a *person*. They just round up some homeless people off the streets for you; nobody misses them.'

We stared at him, sickened. What he was saying was horrific, but worse than that, it was probably true. Everything was cheap in Asia, and that included human life. It was a conversation I'll never forget, but not for lack of trying. Humankind hadn't evolved much, it seemed, with barbarism just out of sight, like rotten fruit turned to hide the blemish. I drank a lot of beer that night. In that sense, I hadn't evolved much either.

I discovered alcohol as a teenager, and like most adolescents, I had no idea how potent it was until I found out the hard way and ended up vomiting in a flowerbed at a party. Given that I had had an inflamed liver and jaundice at fifteen, drinking alcohol at sixteen was an especially poor choice for my health, but I liked the way it made me feel … once I had learnt to stop drinking before I reached the point of throwing up. (It took a while.)

Cigarettes, on the other hand, were something I was always fascinated with. My great-grandfather Jack was the first smoker I can recall meeting and there are photos of him sitting on an upturned milk pail in our backyard, smoking with his legs crossed. Also in the picture is a four-year-old me with a head full of blond curls and a serious expression, sitting on an upturned bucket beside him, attempting to cross my legs and mimic his every action. It wasn't much of a shock, to me, that I became a smoker as an adult.

In the 'un-medicated years' before Zoloft, I administered alcohol and cigarettes to myself freely. The alcohol was a release valve and the hangovers were mild; cigarettes were a little more sinister. I knew that they were bad for me but I didn't care, and when I was feeling particularly dark of thought, I considered each cigarette a tiny suicide, a gesture that reflected my inner turmoil. Eventually, though, and long after I had success with Zoloft, I was just horribly addicted to nicotine and all the other chemicals contained in a Marlboro. I didn't stop smoking until I was thirty-five, when I could feel myself growing short of breath and it scared me, but the other habit established in my late teens, drinking when upset, is deeply ingrained, trumping my own best interests.

Sometimes I think my contrariness is an asset, because whenever I veer too far in one direction, up or down, dark or light, I reach some sort of critical mass and the pendulum starts to swing in the opposite direction. If I'm beginning to believe that I can fly, for instance, my wings vanish, and if I go to bed unable to think of a single thing that's good in the world and profoundly disgusted by the human race, I'll wake up in a really great mood for no discernible reason.

Nothing had changed while I was sleeping; the world was still a vicious place where homeless people were used as targets for sport, dogs were eaten and children were exploited, but I woke up on our last day in Vietnam feeling unreasonably cheerful.

We boarded a 'luxury' coach outside our hotel and found, for once, that the adjective was warranted. Seated vertically in plush seats with airconditioning that worked at an appropriate level, cool but not frigid, we were driven to the Mekong Delta, our Vietnamese tour guide, Fong, loudly informing us in broken English of any notable sights during the ninety-minute journey.

After planes, trains, automobiles and cyclos, we were about to take our chances on a boat. The water taxi that ferried us across the river had a motor and lifejackets, but not so the wooden boats we transferred to, which were predictably rickety and presented a much greater potential for capsizing. If I *did* somehow end up in the caramel-coloured water, it wouldn't matter if I had a lifejacket on or not because I'd die of a heart attack before I drowned. Anything could have been hiding in there.

Gliding down narrow waterways underneath a canopy of coconut palms, the scenery was reminiscent of *Apocalypse Now*, and although tranquil, it was unnervingly easy to imagine snipers hidden in the greenery and bullets whizzing by our heads like they would have during the war. But we had arrived forty years after the event and I had no capacity to grasp what had actually occurred.

Back on the bus in the late afternoon, our appreciative guide chose the medium of song as a special thank-you for joining him on the tour. As we reached the outskirts of the city, he serenaded us over the microphone, bastardising Ronan Keating's ballad 'When You Say Nothing At All' like it had never been bastardised before. If I happen to hear that song now, I don't feel the contempt for Ronan Keating that once burnt like a urinary tract infection: I feel happy because it reminds me of Vietnam, and the dulcet tones of Fong.

7   I ♥ Bangkok

Renee and I had a hot date with the Kingdom of Cambodia, so having bid a fond farewell to Eileen we boarded a bus in Ho Chi Minh City, bound for the Cambodian capital of Phnom Penh. This time around it was a bus of the strictly non-sleeping variety, but just as motorbikes in Vietnam were designed for one or two passengers and carried as many as six or seven, our bus was a sardine can, and when all the seats were taken the bus driver began to stack the aisle with plastic garden chairs, so that we were sitting five abreast like little ducks all in a row. If the bus crashed or caught on fire, then we were going to perish in our seats because there was no way to get out and not enough elbow room to muster the necessary force that would be required to break a window and escape. I don't know why we were surprised. If there was a space in Vietnam that a person could fit into, even barely, then you put a person in it. Needless to say, it was a snug ride.

Shortly after crossing over the border into Cambodia there was a noticeable change in the landscape. Where Vietnam was densely populated and the highway was lined with roadside stalls, Cambodia had space, greenery and much quieter roads. A lot of the homes in Vietnam were rudimentary cement blocks, but some of the dwellings we saw driving to Phnom Penh were nothing more than huts and the asphalt road soon disappeared, to be replaced by potholed dirt roads. It felt like we were stepping back in time. There was more than one scooter on the road with a pig strapped to the back, and sometimes more than one pig, and occasionally twenty chickens. We had barely acclimatised to Vietnam, and now Cambodia was presenting us with another tier of culture shock.

After spending the best part of a day on the bus, we arrived in Phnom Penh and were dropped off at the exotically ornate buildings of the National Museum and the Royal Palace, impressive examples of Khmer architecture. We were staying nearby in a decidedly *un*impressive building, a guesthouse amidst run-down apartment blocks, but it wasn't far to the river or to the hordes of noisy, smiling kids who bum-rushed tourists for money, tugging at their arms or clothes as they begged for dollars.

Compared to Ho Chi Minh City, Phnom Penh felt relaxed and sleepy. It was difficult to reconcile the placid surroundings we were seeing with genocide, but then it's difficult to reconcile anything with genocide.

I was born in 1975, or 'Year Zero' as the communist Khmer Rouge decreed when they seized control of

Cambodia after years of civil war. If you're a maniac who wants to create a new society in line with your ideology, then you might follow the lead of Pol Pot, a former schoolteacher turned Khmer Rouge leader, who saw Cambodia as somebody else's bad poetry, or a burnt cake, and decided that the best course of action was to just tear it up, throw it out, and start again.

The Maoist Khmer Rouge envisioned a rural utopia, a classless agrarian nation of peasants farming the land. So, the de-industrialisation of Cambodia began with the destruction of currency, private property, hospitals, schools, banks, libraries, government buildings and temples, and the forcible evacuation of all citizens to the country to start work. Anyone who was deemed a threat to the 'purity' of the new state was eliminated. Intellectuals, professionals, artists, teachers, lawyers, those with links to the West or to the former government, and even people who wore glasses, were executed and dumped in mass graves throughout the country. Children were taken from their families, put in work camps and told that the state was their family now, or killed so they wouldn't grow up to avenge the death of their murdered parents. By 1980, one-quarter of Cambodia's entire population, around two million people, were dead – murdered by the Khmer Rouge or dying from famine and disease.

Learning about this tragic period of Cambodia's history was extremely confronting, but it felt disrespectful not to educate ourselves about it. After we spent a day exploring the beautiful grounds of the Royal Palace and its colourful, decorative temples, we found a driver to take us to the Tuol Sleng Genocide Museum, a suburban high school that was utilised as a Khmer Rouge execution centre, and the Choeung Ek Killing Fields. With words like 'genocide' and 'killing' in the titles, we expected they would be terrible, but *nothing* could have prepared us for what we saw: the walls and walls of haunting photographic portraits of each prisoner murdered at Tuol Sleng; the towering memorial stupa at the entrance to the Killing Fields stacked with hundreds of human skulls retrieved from the site; and the visible shards of human bone and fragments of clothing still buried in the dirt around the grounds.

A holiday in Cambodia was always going to be a far cry from a holiday spent at Disneyland, unless Disneyland also left you feeling physically sickened, despondent and mentally crushed, but it was a humbling experience, and made me feel grateful for the circumstances of my own life. Cambodia was a wake-up call like no other; except for Auschwitz, Hiroshima, Darfur, Rwanda, Srebrenica … Really, it's amazing that *only* one in four people have depression when we live in a world like this.

With our faith in humanity dashed, we travelled on to Siem Reap to see the spectacular Angkor Wat and Angkor Thom ruins. After the shock of Phnom Penh, it felt soothing to see these ancient temples infiltrated by trees and vines as nature reclaimed its own. Gangs of kids hovered outside the temple gates, selling bracelets and bottles of water to a captive market.

The temple scenery was dramatic, and became even

more so when the weather suddenly turned at the end of a very hot day. In less than a minute a monsoon storm steamrolled the clear blue sky to dark grey, and by the time we had run across the bridge from Angkor Wat to the cover of a waiting tuk-tuk, we were drenched. As we climbed in, a lightning strike hit the ground so close to us that we actually felt the earth move and screamed at the deafening crack. It brought back one of my earliest memories, when our dad took us out golfing and a thunderstorm had appeared when we were out in the middle of the golf course. We were without an umbrella, so my dad in his infinite wisdom made us shelter under the only tree on the green, maximising our chances of electrocution. I think I inherited my outdoor skills from him, too.

The rain continued pouring down on the way back to Siem Reap, turning the dirt roads to mud before we reached our hotel. We were staying in the tourist hub, the part of town populated with markets, bars, restaurants and nightclubs to make visitors feel more at home, or just appealing to those who were drawn to budget hedonism and cheap massages. If you stayed within the perimeters of the Western entertainment strip, you could have been at a happy hour anywhere in the world that sold potent cocktails for a dollar. It was the small children wandering alone through the bar in the early hours of the morning, selling roses and sitting in strangers' laps who reminded you where you were, and that it was a very poor country. And when you drove for ten minutes in any direction from 'Pub Street' you were on dirt roads again, travelling past thatched shacks with no electricity or running water as children wandered by the side of the road, kicking the dirt.

From Cambodia, we flew to Laos, and met Darren at Vientiane airport the next day, collecting him in a clapped-out tuk-tuk. Renee and I felt like we had been away for six months by then, and had been growing travel-weary, and weary of each other, because no matter how much you like someone, three weeks in each other's company, day in and day out, is more than enough. After a while, travelling with a friend tends to take on the bickering quality of a sibling relationship, with one crucial omission – the permission to relieve tension by screaming at each other, safe in the knowledge that you will be forgiven. There is a veil of politeness in friendship, however shabbily it is upheld, that upsets the natural order of things, and while Renee and I did have time apart, it wasn't as cathartic as a fight would have been. Darren's arrival was a boost for our flagging spirits because Cambodia was beautiful, but tragic and emotionally wearing, and having someone new to talk to was refreshing. Our options for conversation had doubled.

Laos seemed calm and chilled, and it was especially so in Luang Prabang, a charming World Heritage-listed riverside town that was home to orange-robed monks, more temples, coffee houses and a whole lot of frangipanis. The most exciting thing that happened in our entire time in Laos was Darren promptly electrocuting himself when he plugged in an appliance. He spent the first twenty-four hours looking ultra alert, as if he'd had six double espressos, and with the hairs on his arms standing on end.

Darren's stay in Laos was actually bookended by near-death experiences, and while I'm not saying he's the archangel of death, I'm not saying he isn't. The Lao Airlines flight we took from Luang Prabang to Chiang Mai in Thailand a week later was a white-knuckle thrill ride through the mountains on an airline with an atrocious air safety record, something we'd checked when we saw the plane and immediately regretted doing. Google had helped us to find clean hotels, tasty food and a waterfall, but now it had turned on us. And the flight didn't disappoint, with some wild turbulence enhanced by broken seatbelts.

Fear is quite a drug. High in the sky and afraid that I wouldn't be for much longer I cleared the air with the universe and any deities that might have been listening: *You know how I said I wished I was dead, back on that overnight bus in Vietnam? And that suicide attempt at fifteen? I take it all back! I didn't mean it! PLEASE LET ME LIVE!*

We dropped altitude abruptly at one point, and I'm pretty sure our souls left an imprint on the roof of the plane before the pilot managed to recover our course, or possibly woke up from his nap. When we got off the plane, Darren kissed the ground.

Now that we were in Thailand, the land of delicious curries, soups and the stickiest of rices, we decided to do a cooking class. After shopping for our ingredients at a local market, we returned to our 'cooking stations' in the kitchen, put on our aprons and chopped an assortment of vegetables, chicken and fresh herbs. All of our ingredients were prepped without any drama and everything was going perfectly well until a live flame was introduced to the mix.

'We need lots of heat! Turn gas high, *high*!' our Thai chef instructed us. There were about fifteen students in the room, so with each wok turned on maximum power, the small, un-airconditioned room began to heat up. We started to sweat.

'Okay! Oil is nice and hot. Add chicken!' he yelled. 'Watch out; little fire!'

My wok was starting to smoke, and the chicken dish contained some liquid, so when I added it there wasn't a 'little fire' as we had been warned. A giant fireball exploded out of my wok, and if I had been leaning in any closer, I would have cremated my face. As it was, I'd only burnt my finger, but everybody screamed when they saw the huge flame. I wasn't the only one to cause a scene. I saw another girl ask her boyfriend hopefully, 'Is it bad? How bad is it?' She had successfully singed her eyebrows and her fringe, but her boyfriend was bent over with laughter and couldn't speak. Even above all the fragrant spices you could still smell burning hair.

We got to eat the dishes we had made afterwards and the food tasted delicious, perhaps more so because none of us required a skin graft for our kitchen injuries. That old saying, 'Give a man a fish and you feed him for a day; teach a man to fish and you feed him for a lifetime' was the thinking behind our cooking class enrolment. Teach us how to make curry, and we won't have to order takeaway anymore, and although we all remarked how much it easier it was to cook Pad Thai and red and green curries than we'd thought and *said* that we'd go home and cook them ourselves, none of us could ever be assed.

There's never been a more aptly named city than Bangkok, although Tastynoodles would have worked, too. I'm not sure whose idea it was, but after drinking beer on Khaosan Road for several hours like every other unimaginative tourist in town, Renee, Darren and I crammed into a tuk-tuk, uttered the magic words 'ping-pong', and ended up at a sex show in the notorious red light district of Patpong. It was one of the infamous attractions of Bangkok and something we felt we had to do, despite a hunch that it was going to be a little too much 'reality' for us and that we'd end up watching the show through our fingers. They were known as ping-pong shows because the women were famous for shooting ping-pong balls out of their vaginas, but there was *so* much more to it than that according to the twenty-five item 'menu'.

The small stage in the middle of the room was surrounded by rows of benches, like a very small theatre, and on the stage were some of the most talented vaginas in Thailand. They were clever enough to write 'Welcome to Bangkok!' on a postcard, cavernous enough to hold a very long feather boa and garlands of plastic flowers, and powerful enough to shoot darts at balloons and send ping-pong balls whizzing across the room. When one woman's genitals regurgitated a live goldfish into a bowl, Darren understandably dropped his beer, and it smashed all over the cement floor.

'I'm from *Lismore!*' he said, by way of explanation. (Lismore is his home town in country New South Wales where presumably goldfish aren't so readily subjected to snatch abuse.)

Every couple of party tricks there was a change of pace and a naked couple appeared onstage. The couple moved through a karma sutra of sex positions, their facial expressions like those of someone completing a tax return *and* discovering they wouldn't be getting much of a refund. These were called 'sex shows', not sexy shows, which was an important distinction since there was nothing sexy about it. If anything, it felt like being at a weird circus, and that went for the audience, too. There were young, drunk men, middle-aged couples, a group of three women in burkas and us, looking like we were *all* from Lismore.

After all that hard work, being poked and prodded and flipped in the air, the vagina smoked a cigarette and Darren's second beer smashed to the floor.

'Cut it out!' I told him. 'These beers cost almost as much as our hotel.'

And they did, because the ping-pong people were going to squeeze the money out of you somehow, just like that poor goldfish had been squeezed out of that woman's nether regions. You could either get ripped off at the door paying a hefty entrance fee, or a ransom to get your passport back when you left, or you could watch the show for 'free' but the price of drinks was ridiculously bloated and drinking was compulsory, not just because the people at the show said so but also because you needed some sort of liquid anaesthesia to impair your vision. No matter how much money these women ended up getting in their hand, or their vagina, at the end of the night, it was never going to be compensation enough.

Darren went to the bathroom and came back looking even more shaken and incredulous.

'I just got asked if I wanted a threesome with two lady-boys for *three* Australian dollars.'

'How could you tell they were ladyboys?' we asked him.

'Uh, because their dicks were hanging out,' he replied.

The menu, played through once in its entirety, started again, so the vaginas were doing the same tricks on hourly rotation for however long the place stayed open. That couldn't be good for you, or the goldfish. And our complicity in paying to observe this spectacle meant that we were now part of a much larger problem and had done our small part to contribute to the downfall of civilisation. When we left I didn't know if it was more appropriate to laugh or cry, but we were drunk and flying through the Bangkok traffic into the night in a tuk-tuk, so we sang instead, a little Ronan Keating for old time's sake. Then we ate one-dollar Pad Thai on the street and passed out cold.

The other thing we did in Bangkok, besides drinking, eating and disappointing our parents by attending a sex show, was shop. Goods were cheap there, and we were too, so we attacked the market stalls in a frenzy, like kids who had just smashed their piggy bank open with a hammer.

A wooden frog that makes a frog noise when you drag a stick across its back? A cumbersome lamp that'll be a nightmare to transport? And if I buy five of your t-shirts, you'll throw in one for free? PLEASE SIR, TAKE MY MONEY!

We may as well have just walked through the market throwing Baht notes at people, or setting them on fire, which is exactly what happened to the lamp I bought when I finally got it home to Australia and plugged it in. Darren had a little more success with the one he purchased. His just gave him a nasty electric shock every time he turned it on or off.

Darren and Renee were both much more diligent about travelling to Asia than I was, so they were taking doxy-cycline, the anti-malaria medication, in case they were attacked by disease-carrying mosquitoes, while I took my usual approach of flying by the seat of my pants. In the event that we were attacked by a swarm of malarial mosquitoes, I would certainly be sorry I wasn't better prepared, but in terms of punishing adverse reactions to medication, I was spared. Renee had had 'digestive issues' since Cambodia and Darren developed photosensitivity, both potential side effects of doxycycline when taken at doses high enough to fend off malaria. Renee saw more than her fair share of squat toilets and couldn't afford to be choosy about which ones, while Darren turned bright red after spending ten minutes outdoors without sunscreen and resembled a tomato that had grown a torso, arms and legs. I was also red, but that's just because my skin is pasty and fries like bacon no matter how much sunscreen I slap on it or how often. So the three of us, and all our ridiculous market purchases, left Bangkok on an overnight train, looking a little worse for wear and a lot like we were moving house.

The trains in Thailand were a little less ghetto than the Vietnamese ones, and we all managed to sleep soundly. Darren slept a little *too* soundly, rolling on top of his new digital camera in the night and shattering the screen into splinters. That was the premature end for 'Camera #1'. It had had a lifespan of just three days.

'Camera #2' fared better and made it through our time on the island of Koh Samui. It captured many priceless moments, including Darren lying on the chaise lounge that furnished our room and imploring us, like Kate Winslet did in *Titanic*, to 'Draw me like one of your French girls!' And it also memorialised us enjoying cocktails in glasses as big as fishbowls while watching a very entertaining ladyboy cabaret show. Its next job was to document our time on the Phi Phi Islands.

It took quite a long time for us to get to Koh Phi Phi (pronounced Pee Pee), and involved a bus, a ferry, a minibus and a dubious-looking boat from the port of Krabi. The boat had a disturbing lack of lifejackets and flotation devices – items that were probably considered too space-consuming, especially since their absence meant that you could jam more people inside the boat. Perhaps those additional people were really good at holding their breath for an extended period and could be used for flotation if the boat sank? In any case, I'm sure the people in charge had a well-rehearsed disaster plan so we wouldn't end up as fish food, but I crossed my fingers and sent a shout-out to St Jude, hope of the hopeless and my mum's favourite saint, asking that we wouldn't sink. When we finally docked at the port in Phi Phi we felt the same sense of relief that we had after our Lao Airlines flight, which wasn't so much flying across the sky as being flung.

Our first impression of Koh Phi Phi Don, the largest island with all the accommodation, was that it could just as easily have been called Koh Poo Poo Don because the area we walked through on the way to our hotel smelt like a broken toilet. The island was in remarkable shape, though, considering that the majority of its infrastructure had been decimated by the Indian Ocean tsunami just a few years earlier. The blue and white 'Tsunami Evacuation Route' signs posted around the island were a chilling reminder. Perhaps partly in light of that disaster, we had booked a hilltop hotel, splurging a little extra on fancier accommodation for our last few nights.

From our balcony, you could look out over the bright blue water to Koh Phi Phi Leh, the smaller, undeveloped island that was sort of like our island's naturally beautiful younger sister and was famous for being the place where *The Beach* was filmed. Koh Phi Phi Don was beautiful, too, but development, noisy bars and litter had modified its looks. It was the girl who had got breast implants, Botox and collagen with the intention of increasing her beauty, but had ended up looking generic instead. Koh Phi Phi

Don was overdeveloped like a lot of other tropical islands catering to tourists. Perhaps if people like us were prepared to stay in tents or thatched huts and didn't demand the amenities of home, it may not have become so.

As we sat on the beach the next morning after breakfast, checking out the view, one of our fellow guests was getting a two-dollar foot massage and complaining of the nearby construction, 'I wish they would just leave nature *alone*!' as if our hotel had been sculpted out of seagull shit or had washed up on the shore like an enormous piece of seaweed. She was probably the sort of tourist who said things like, 'This place would be GREAT if it wasn't for all the TOURISTS,' but you can't have your Thai fishcake and eat it, too.

The main activities on Phi Phi appeared to be either aquatic (scuba diving, snorkelling and swimming), or alcoholic – the opportunity to literally drink booze by the bucket load was advertised at most of the beachside bars.

Alcohol is cheap in Asia. It's a little *too* cheap if you know what I mean, and does nothing to dissuade one from taking up healthier pastimes, such as drinking coconut juice, making a bra from empty coconut shells or going fishing. We had taken advantage of our proximity to cheap beer throughout our trip, but after almost six weeks away the novelty was wearing thin.

The part of drinking where you're drunk or becoming so is always enjoyable for me, and sometimes I think that the only thing I've mastered in life is achieving happiness through alcohol. It's a self-defeating act in the long term (and in the morning) but while Zoloft has had a beneficial effect on my mental health and emotional stamina, it has done much less for my tendency to self-harm in subtle, socially acceptable ways. Although it's unwise, I often take the lazy person's route to makeshift lightness and ease. I like myself when I'm drunk, in fact I think I'm pretty great, and if nobody else does, *I don't care.* That's what I like best about it; it makes me care less. Drinking is an airbag of happiness, a comforting cushion, when life feels like a car crash. And the cost of alcohol in terms of dollars is nothing compared with the feeling it brings, from my glass to God's ear. So those are the positive, fleeting attributes of alcohol. The negative ones come afterwards, when the alcohol has worn off and I wake up with a mouth as dry as a sand burrito, a head full of ache, a phone full of weird texts, black holes in my memory, no money in my wallet, a low mood and a general malaise that makes me fit only for watching television and eating greasy takeaway food on the couch. The 'best me' that I *think* I am when I'm drinking doesn't have much to say the morning after.

Darren, Renee and I decided to avoid the bucket cocktail route, as tempting as drinking from a *bucket* sounded, and stuck to bottled water and Tiger beer. It was too easy to see ourselves succumbing to alcohol poisoning, or straight-up poisoning, and we were a long way from a proper hospital, a place we wished to avoid if humanly possible. Soon enough we would all be back at work and spending forty hours a week in one.

Our time on holiday was ticking down, as were our funds, so we cut as many corners as we could while trying our best not to be insensitive jerks. The beach near our hotel was lined with long-tail boats (Thai fishing boats powered by car engines with a distinctive long-shaft propeller) that were used to taxi tourists around the island and out to reefs for diving or snorkelling. If you were cheap or broke, they could also to take you over to Koh Phi Phi Leh, in lieu of one of the bigger, more luxurious cruise boats. We were those cheap people.

After negotiating a reasonable price with one of the fishermen, we climbed into the boat, which was decorated with a wreath of colourful flowers, and headed out into the bay. From our hotel room, and even from the beach, the water looked calm, but further out it became *very* choppy, and as the boat rose and fell in the water, my breakfast almost did the same. Our boat driver nonchalantly smoked a cigarette with one hand, and steered with the other while we held on to the sides by our fingernails, trying not to be launched off the wooden seat every time we went over a wave and screaming involuntarily when there was a particularly large one.

Eventually we reached a more sheltered spot, which was still a little choppy but much calmer than the journey over. To our surprise, the driver dropped anchor.

'You swim,' he told us.

'What? Where's the beach?' I asked, confused. The turquoise water in this cove was beautiful but it wasn't Maya Bay, it wasn't *the* beach.

'You swim,' the driver repeated.

'No, we want to go to *Maya Bay*,' Renee explained. 'The *beach*.' Something had obviously been lost in translation.

'No boat go; you swim. There!' he said, throwing his cigarette butt into the water and pointing at a large opening in the base of the rock wall. 'Beach there!'

'Oh, *shit*!'

We looked at one another. This was not what we had expected. If we'd known we were going to have to *swim* to the beach, we would have worn swimwear instead of clothes.

'For camera!' the driver said, offering us plastic bags and a bigger insulated, waterproof bag to put our things in. This was happening, whether we liked it or not.

'Okay, I'll take the bag,' Darren said, moving into action mode, so we each wrapped our cameras in a plastic shopping bag, tied a tight knot, and then put them inside the bigger bag.

'Are you sure it's sealed properly?' Renee asked worriedly.

'Yeah, I think so. I *hope* so,' Darren replied.

We argued about who was going to go first, took off our shoes and one by one jumped over the side of the boat. We flailed about in the water, giggling as we tried to swim through the surprisingly strong current with our shoes in our hands, just as one of the big, flashy tour boats passed by so that everyone on board could point and laugh at us and ensure our humiliation was complete.

Getting through the water to the rock was one thing, but we hadn't considered the coral reef leading up to the rock.

'OUCH! OW! FUCK!' we yelled as we shredded our hands and knees on the sharp coral. It felt like trying to climb a cheese grater.

All safely at the top of the rocky outcrop, though out of breath and bleeding from various cuts and scrapes, we made our way through the opening in the cliff and walked down a short path to 'the beach', which was congested with a hundred other tourists, none of whom were actively bleeding like us, as far as we could tell, and had obviously chosen to travel by one of the five enormous cruise boats moored in the water. It looked less like a tropical paradise and more like a marina, but we'd put in too much effort to get there, so we were still going to take a shitload of photos of it all.

'Can I have my camera?' Renee asked, and Darren untied the top of the bag and stuck his hand into a puddle.

'*Motherfucker!*' he shouted. 'Camera #2', the replacement he had bought after crushing 'Camera #1', was swimming inside the plastic shopping bag, and Renee's camera was dripping wet as well. Mine was the only camera that miraculously had managed to stay dry.

'Maybe they'll still work,' I said, feeling survivor's guilt, 'if you try turning them on?'

But they didn't.

'*FUCK!*' Darren complained angrily. 'I've wrecked *TWO* CAMERAS in *ONE HOLIDAY.*'

'You've wrecked *three*,' Renee said bitterly.

All in all, it wasn't the most successful outing.

I have no memory of how we got back to the boat for our ride home, or how we managed to climb aboard without it capsizing, but I'm sure it was graceless and undignified. The only thing I remember is sailing back to Kho Phi Phi Don, with Renee and Darren both seething and holding their broken cameras.

'We'll laugh about this one day!' I shouted over the sound of the waves and the putt-putt of the engine, and they both looked at me, the one with a functioning camera, like I had farted.

I suppose it was too soon.

8   Höllenloch

I used to think that the longer I was away from home, the better. Why go travelling anywhere for two weeks if I could travel for two months? Why eat one slice of cake if you could eat three? The prospect of diabetes and a fast track to a Fatogram career hadn't yet deterred me from overeating, and gorging on travel wasn't like gorging on cake; it gave you fresh eyes, not cellulite. It was good for you. But the longer you're away, the harder it is to come back.

After six weeks in Asia, I was back at the hospital, and the patients who were okay before I left were now dying, and the ones who were dying had died. I knew when I took a job working with cancer patients that people would die, but after two years I felt I was losing my emotional resilience. Deaths were affecting me more as time went by, not less, and the effects of grief were compounding. If I wasn't physically away from the hospital, I was trying to get further away from it by drinking.

Holiday withdrawal, much like alcohol or drug withdrawal, can most easily be alleviated by administering more of the same, although doing so means that you become trapped in a cycle of constant craving instead of addressing the underlying issue. My pattern was to return to work after a holiday and immediately, compulsively, begin planning the next one, instead of examining the fine print of my life and recognising that perhaps my job wasn't such a good fit for me. It was never so much a holiday as fleeing the scene.

True to form, within three days of returning to work I had applied for an extended period of leave, and so had Renee, who shared my post-holiday slump. Darren was bummed, too, perhaps even more than we were because he had very little recreation leave to access, but he planned to use whatever he *did* have by joining Renee and me on another holiday posthaste. As travel companions, we made a successful team. It had only taken a few days of wholesale personal space, sleeping in our own beds and returning to work to dissolve any residual contempt from overexposure, to reaffirm our bond of friendship and fire up future travel plans. Thus, our previous record of six weeks in Asia would be eclipsed by a four-month international odyssey encompassing Japan, Europe and the United States. What Renee and I failed to realise in the giddy, ambitious, planning stage, was that after about three weeks, and certainly after six, a holiday doesn't really feel like a holiday anymore. It starts to feel like a job, or an unpaid internship, with responsibilities that include locating reasonable food sources, sanitary accommodation and the direction north, as you make your way around unfamiliar terrain. But I was adamant, then, that more travel equalled more enjoyment and nobody could tell me otherwise. When I was a kid I believed that a rabbit brought chocolate eggs to my house and that buses with those accordion bits in the middle played music when they went around a corner. Things change.

In order to finance my newest adventure, I worked eight months of twelve-hour night shifts, like someone allergic to sunlight, socialisation and mood stability, and it did nothing to assist my dwindling ability to cope with the intensity of my workplace. I had never really *wanted* to come back to the oncology ward after any of my prior trips overseas (I don't know anyone who relishes the prospect of returning to work) but this time I had a vague feeling that I actually *wouldn't* be. I was setting the wheels of change in motion, albeit in subtle ways. The lease of my apartment had expired three months before I was due to leave and I took the liberty of staying with my brother, Michael, in the interim, to save money and keep my options open. He was also an oncology nurse and had his own flat, one he shared with his young daughter, Ciara … and me, for far longer than was reasonable. But both Michael and Ciara were used to having me around. We had shared a house together in Brisbane for a few years, and when Michael had custody of Ciara on weekends and holidays, I got to see her, too. I was just part of the furniture to her, maybe an unstable table, but she was much more to me.

Although I felt like a maniac working permanent nights, with periodic fits of tears and rage that exceeded hormonal parameters, my relationship with Dave was still going strong and, like Darren, he had decided to join Renee and me for part of our trip. But unlike Darren, it was going to be for two months and not two weeks. I knew that I could travel with Darren and Renee, because I had done it before, I was going to do it again and we were all still friends, but I wasn't as confident about the travelling-with-a-boyfriend part. My prior attempt had been a learning curve, which is really just a gentler way of saying a mistake, but being apart for four months seemed worse than spending two months together and having things go pear-shaped.

I dare anyone to *not* have a good time on holiday in Japan, because that was exactly what we had as we zipped across the country on super-fast trains for two weeks, visiting magnificent temples, castles and seizure-inducing neon cities. An abundance of bright red autumn leaves made all our photos effortlessly impressive, and the weather was chilly but tolerable for a gang of soft Australians. It was during our second week in Japan that the teething problems and squabbling began. Darren and Renee bickered like children and Dave and I sniped at one another, which escalated to a stupid fight that ended with us not speaking.

We had been away for ten days.

When it was time for Darren to fly back to Australia, he was envious of our travel itinerary, but relieved that he wouldn't be travelling with us.

Next on the itinerary was two weeks in Norway, where we descended on the generous, saintly family of friends, and except for the part where I drank moonshine, thought I could rap and woke up on the floor, starfish-style in my underwear with the worst hangover of my life, it was wonderful. For poor Renee, stuck travelling with a couple, and one that managed to turn an evening of ice-skating into a verbal stoush, it wasn't quite so fantastic, but Norway was a beautiful country, the smoked salmon was dreamy and the tap-water tasted like Evian. The same could not be said for the tap-water in London, our next destination. It tasted ... *preloved*.

Since I had last seen my sister in 2006 she and her boyfriend, Tony, had got married. We spent Christmas in London with her and her new in-laws, eating a lot and drinking more, and the next day we all went to Prague and Berlin for a week; just Tony, Jo, Dave, Renee and me, like one big ad hoc family. It was a holiday within a holiday for us, and an unofficial, very unromantic honeymoon for Jo and Tony. Jo was ill from food poisoning, and Tony shit himself whenever anyone said, 'Mrs Walkley', looking around, alarmed, for his mother.

It was the first time I'd been back to the Czech Republic since the hedonistic, manic days of 1999 and it hadn't changed a lot in ten years, but my brain certainly had. Prague was still beautiful, cobblestoned and heavy on the dumplings, but this visit was a much more subdued affair than my first, except for the part right at the end when we arranged for someone to take us to the train station for twenty dollars, and that someone turned out to be a maniac. When another car dared to cut us off in traffic, our driver went berserk with road rage, ran a red light and started chasing the other car across the city, in the opposite direction to the train station. We ended up driving in a huge loop before arriving at the station with a minute to spare before our train to Berlin departed, and found that our pre-agreed cab fare had suddenly quintupled. If we weren't willing to cough up the cash, the driver seemed more than willing to beat it out of us because he was evidently a *fucking lunatic*, so we paid him, resentfully, and ran like hell for the train, just making it.

The hotel we had booked in Kreuzberg, Berlin, was the only available accommodation left in the city on New Year's Eve that could fit our party of five, and, to my delight, a 'continental buffet breakfast' was included in the price. If a hotel has the words 'buffet' and 'breakfast' anywhere within its spectrum of services, then I am going to stay there above other hotels, even ones with swimming pools and really nice shampoo and conditioner, because there's nothing like the prospect of a big, all-you-can-eat spread to make me lose my mind. And when I go to breakfast, I go to *town*, because even if you've already paid for it, a buffet still feels like a free meal and an opportunity you should take advantage of. My friend Shaun has a food-related phobia, where foods of a certain colour are not allowed to touch foods of another colour, and if he saw the unholy chaos on my plate when I'm cutting loose at a buffet, he would shit twice and die. I have a little bit of everything, because I can't make a decision to save my life, and at a buffet, I don't have to. It's a style of dining that suits me.

I believe that breakfast is a meal you eat before midday, after which time it becomes brunch, lunch, dinner or supper, depending on how long after midday it is that you're eating, so when we walked into the lobby of our Berlin hotel at 4 p.m. to check in, I was surprised to see that the 'continental buffet breakfast' I'd been so excited about was still sitting out in a corner of the room. Presumably it had been there all day, uncovered and open to the elements, which was disconcerting to say the least. Much more troubling, however, was seeing an older man, perhaps a fellow hotel guest, perhaps a starving hobo, standing before the buffet perusing the culinary offerings and also *tasting them* – sticking the serving spoons in his mouth, licking them clean and then putting them back into the food. His spit was added to a dish of tuna, a tray of scrambled egg, a bowl of fruit salad and then, as my sister and I watched in nauseated horror, he dipped his fingers repeatedly into each of the condiments.

'Have you eaten at a buffet lately?' I asked Jo. 'Because that's probably how you got food poisoning.'

The buffet dream was dead.

After we'd paid in full, the hotel manager informed us that our room wasn't quite ready because our beds were still being made, but that we were welcome to go in and drop off our bags if we wished. Having worked as a maid, I took that to mean the bed linen was being changed and the finishing touches were being put on the room, such as folding the end of the toilet paper into a point to give you the welcoming gift of a stranger's hand-germs to wipe on your intimate bits.

The manager instructed another employee to show us to our room. We followed him through the part of the hotel we'd seen online then out of the hotel altogether, through a car park and into another building that was somewhat removed from the hotel itself. The manager was right, our beds *were* being made – two men with hammers and planks of wood were constructing rows of Ikea bunk beds for us to sleep in. The room was huge, which could have been a good thing except that it was draughty and cold, had no heating and there was a ratty old bedsheet nailed to the wall for a curtain. The only hotel in Berlin with a vacancy didn't *really* have a vacancy after all; it had just opened up a shed for us to sleep in.

Before we saw the room in the flesh, we'd all agreed that it didn't really matter what it was like because we were only going to be sleeping there for a couple of nights, which is what you tell yourself when you're not expecting too much from your accommodation. If a hotel's shit, the only thing you'll *want* to do there is sleep, but if it's really shit, you won't even want to do that. This *Höllenloch*, German for 'hellhole', was so bad that if we had any other option, we would have pissed ourselves laughing and left, but there was nowhere else to go because it was New Year's Eve, everywhere was full, snow was forecast, and we had already paid. The array of dismayed facial expressions was amazing. Collectively, we looked like someone forced to do an urgent poo in a new love interest's studio apartment, only to discover, upon successful bowel evacuation, that the toilet was broken and the secret brown shame wouldn't flush. The *horror*.

'I'm pretty sure this place was a prison once,' Jo said, 'like, yesterday.'

My sister has a heart of gold but she can be quite the ball-breaker when she wants to be, so she stomped back out to the manager to tear him a new asshole and demand that he find us alternative lodgings. Our room was terrible, even though it cost almost as much per night as the better rooms in the hotel that appeared to have curtains, central heating and assembled furniture, but he had us over a barrel and he knew it.

Jo came back fifteen minutes later, fuming.

'There's nowhere else we can stay, but they're going to bring us a heater and give us a *partial* refund.'

We all groaned. Just then there was a knock at the door and we were presented with a tiny two-bar radiator as heating, which was laughable considering the size of the room, except we weren't at the stage where we could laugh yet. We were hovering in the emotional no-man's-land between crying and wanting to smash something, and then we saw the communal bathroom.

The showers were wretched, an abomination in terms of both style and function, and partitioned into cubicles with flaking chipboard, which only heightened the overall prison ambience. The plumbing was unfortunately as effective as it looked, as I discovered that evening. By the time

I had finished washing my hair, filmy tepid water, which was rapidly becoming cold, reached halfway to my knees and the chipboard was left with a wet tidemark of filth that would never dry out in the cold, damp air. I needed a shower after having a shower as if I was stuck in an Escher drawing; I could go on showering endlessly here, trying to get clean and never getting anywhere.

When I emerged from the bathroom, shivering and mostly numb, my sister's husband, Tony, was gathering up his toiletries and mentally preparing himself to broach the abysmal amenities.

'How's the shower?' he asked, as if he already knew the answer to the question but was hoping against hope I would tell him he was wrong.

'Don't drop the soap,' I replied.

The good thing about having horrible accommodation in winter is that it gets you out and about. If we had been staying in a hotel that had heat and a television or just didn't feel quite so much like an abandoned asylum, I would have seen a lot less of the freezing city outside, but I probably wouldn't have had to sleep in my clothes.

So, our accommodation wasn't all that we had hoped it would be, sure, but it couldn't detract from the fact that it was New Year's Eve, the night of nights for endorsed binge drinking. We would say, 'Auf wiedersehen!' to 2007 in the city where the Berlin Wall came down and David Hasselhoff, wearing a very sparkly jacket, sang a song celebrating freedom while the world watched in wonder. Brisbane had no such bragging rights.

We walked around the streets of Kreuzberg looking for a restaurant that we could all agree on, a phenomenon almost as rare as a unicorn. There was an atmosphere of excitement, mischief and detonated explosives all around us as someone said, 'Oh, yeah, Thai food!' and someone else said, 'Ugh, I hate coriander.' And my sister pleaded, urgently, 'Please, just pick something soon, anything; I need to go the toilet!' Her voice was by far the most persuasive, so we entered the nearest (Turkish) restaurant.

Something that New Year's Eve in Europe has over the New Year's celebrations in Australia (the ones I've experienced at least) is that the fireworks aren't just up in the night sky, or exploding off the Sydney Harbour Bridge, they're right there in your hot little hands. I love fireworks. They are dangerous, yes, but so is anything you intentionally set on fire in order to watch it explode, as my brother can attest when he almost blew up our shed with his chemistry set, an ill-advised gift for a budding pyromaniac. I think he was ten years old when he decided to do some 'burning off' on the vine that covered the back of our house ... by dousing it with petrol and setting it alight.

Much more dangerous than fireworks themselves, though, is a large number of highly intoxicated people being in possession of them and running amok through a city, as we soon learnt when a firecracker exploded in the doorway of the restaurant we'd chosen, and scared us witless. Maybe we were already skittish, but the explosion took us over the edge and turned us into pious advocates for safety, our bitter complaining punctuated by the loud popping sound of crackers detonating outside. After dinner, we had to make our way to a bar two blocks from the restaurant to meet up with friends and we did not cope well with the chaos. Berlin on New Year's Eve was exploding pyrotechnic nirvana, and hailing from Australia, where fireworks were either severely restricted or illegal, we were grossly unprepared.

'This is LUNACY!' I shouted, as we watched a whistling rocket shoot beneath a tram where it loudly exploded, scattering the road with luminous embers and leaving a cloud of blue-grey smoke and the smell of gunpowder. But like a homophobic politician caught in flagrante with a rent boy, it only took a few drinks in the warm buffer zone of a bar before we began to embrace what we had so vociferously claimed to be against.

By midnight we had taken over a corner of the bar that offered an excellent view of the Straße, a street that now resembled a war zone. When some very drunk, very friendly Germans gave us a handful of fireworks from the arsenal in their backpacks, we did our own small part to contribute to the mayhem, and watched in amused horror as a rocket was sent flying through the open window of an apartment across the street, where it exploded all over someone's living room and probably started a fire.

'THIS IS THE BEST NEW YEAR'S *EVER!*' someone shouted. 'WE SHOULD TOTALLY TRY THIS AT HOME!'

Despite the abundance of missiles in our midst, miraculously none of us were injured, burnt, blinded or even singed during the festivities, but just when we were starting to feel pleased with ourselves, the bar closed and it was time to go back to our shack. We had stayed out for as long as possible, but the excessive alcohol intake meant that everyone else passed out and began dump truck snoring while my brain was still wired and wide awake. Not sufficiently deafened by the fireworks and New Year's related singing and shouting, I heard solo numbers and snored duets and at one stage everyone combined to form an impromptu choir. Unfortunately, the pillow was so thin I couldn't even use it to smother myself.

Although we woke up on New Year's Day to falling snow, we couldn't get out of our room fast enough and only noticed a marginal difference in temperature when we did. We decided to make the most of the bleak day by doing a walking tour of the city, with the added incentive that the walking part might warm us up.

When I first visited Berlin in 1999, the calendar said it was spring, and there might have been flowers blooming and birds singing like crazy all around me but I wouldn't have known because I had my scarf wrapped around my head three times to try and block out the freezing air. Shocked by the weather, I was also struck by how empty the streets were, and how a city of 3.4 million people could manage to seem so quiet.

It was the same again in 2008, although on a legitimately cold New Year's Day it was understandable that not many people were around. A bunch of them were probably in hospital after having their hands and fingers blown off and only people with a hotel room as shit as ours would go out walking for twelve hours when the temperature was so bitterly cold.

'Where are all the people?' I asked the guide as we set off through mostly vacant streets.

'Spain,' she said. 'In the sun.'

Our knowledgeable guide provided us with a running commentary of the city's many notable and notorious landmarks, and a lot of them made me think that if the earth ceased to exist because it was swallowed by a black hole, it wouldn't be such a bad thing, but it was an incredible tour.

'This is where the Nazis burnt all the books,' she told us, and 'This is the site of Hitler's bunker,' and, 'There used to be a statue of an eagle holding a swastika on top of this pillar.'

Bullet holes still peppered the façades of drab apartment buildings and the Brandenburg Gate, yet this horrific narrative was contained in a sprawling modern city with a crane-dotted skyline. Berlin was fascinating in that way; it was a place where you could reach out and touch history with your bare hands and, at the same time, you saw the future surging relentlessly on around it, like water bypassing rocks in a river.

The city in winter was grey, bleak and bitterly cold and I made a note of it, in the event that my depression ever made a serious comeback and demanded a complementary environment, because Berlin in winter looked like being depressed felt. There are places I've been that make me think happy thoughts, like Venice and Baskin Robbins, and other places where I can only envision being miserable and going through life with a face that looked like I was sucking on a lemon. Berlin didn't want me for a sunbeam.

'You know what?' I said to my boyfriend. 'I could see myself living here and being very unhappy.'

'I'm already unhappy here,' he said, blowing on to his frozen fingers through chattering teeth.

When night fell and the temperature dropped further, we were forced to admit that we could no longer feel our legs, so we reluctantly returned to the stalag and endeavoured to thaw out.

'You know what I keep hoping?' I asked Jo, as we sat on our crappy bunk beds trying to read in the dismal lighting.

'That we'll get arrested so we can sleep somewhere else?' she suggested.

'No. I keep hoping that this room is going to be like *Hogan's Heroes* and that there's a trapdoor in the floor under my bed with a tunnel that goes straight to a better hotel.'

'There's not,' she said, bursting my bubble. 'I checked under all the beds to make sure there weren't any rats or wild animals, and there was only chewed up gum and an old comb.'

I shivered. I hadn't considered the possibility of vermin until then.

The following evening we took refuge in a cinema, where there was both entertainment and heat. We were getting good at finding shelter when darkness descended, even if it was subtitled, and spending the majority of time in our accommodation being unconscious, which was ideal.

When we left Berlin after five nights, no one remarked

'Oh, it was so bad it was almost good,' or, 'You know, I think that place was starting to grow on me,' as we might have, but there were still many positives to be found. It was good that we had somewhere indoors to sleep so that we wouldn't die of hypothermia; it was really good that none of the top bunks had concertinaed into the bottom bunks, and it was great that we'd witnessed the man eating at the buffet before we'd had a chance to. And creatively speaking, it was a boon. I could hardly have written so much about eating room service while sitting on a bidet in a penthouse suite at the Hilton.

9 These Pretzels Are Making Me Anxious

After Berlin we spent a fun month visiting the Netherlands, Belgium, Spain, France and Italy, travelling by train and papering over our Höllenloch memories. I know that we visited many memorable cultural landmarks in that time because I have a bunch of photos of them somewhere, but my memory has a cataloguing system where 'Food', 'Drink' and 'Celebrity News' immediately leap to mind instead. There were fries and curried mayonnaise in Amsterdam, churros and sangria in Barcelona, beer and pork ribs in Belgium, and paella and learning of Heath Ledger's death in Valencia. I'm glad the Sistine Chapel and the Colosseum don't have feelings that I could hurt.

When alcohol was added to an extended period of travel with a significant other, it proved to be a combustible mix. Most awkwardly for Renee, there was a shouting match and tears (mine) in the street in Rome and a few other eruptions along the way, but as our time in Europe drew to a close, Dave and I knew each other a lot better, and more importantly, still liked one another enough to plan to move in together when I got back. Things *had* got messy while we were away, as I feared they would, but nothing was broken.

At the end of January, Dave had to fly back to Australia to start a new job and Renee and I began our North America jaunt. I thought we would 'hit' New York, but New York hit me instead. In the moment it felt like something that had come out of the blue, but in retrospect, I had been warming up to a proper meltdown for a while. Eight months of night shift, followed by three months of living out of a bag during a European winter and on a shoestring budget had taken their toll. Being on holiday is a lot more enjoyable than going to work, but it's not without its stressors and I was slowly imploding.

Renee and I had flown from London to New York at the beginning of a freezing February for the final five weeks of our trip. The plan was to spend two weeks in New York City, then carry on to Las Vegas, the Grand Canyon and Los Angeles before our return flight to Australia. The only real danger that we could foresee was potentially running out of money before we got to the finish line, or our constant bickering erupting into a fistfight because we were sick of the sight of each other after eleven weeks. Our relationship as travel companions had begun to feel like a bad marriage. We loved each other, but we both wanted to start seeing other people.

On my first trip to New York in 2006 I had stayed in reasonable hotels, the kind where you had your own bathroom and a door that locked and you didn't have to hide your wallet and passport in your pillowcase while you slept. The accommodation wasn't anything special, but it was private and comfortable. Well, those swell days were *over*.

With dwindling funds, our home away from home this time around was on the fourth floor of a five-storey walk-up, a hostel called 'Jazz on the Park'. In name alone, it was the accommodation of my nightmares. I hate hostels and I hate jazz, but if you're like me and have what is known in the accounting business as 'shit for brains', then you can't really complain when you end up sleeping in a dormitory with eight bunk beds crammed into it because you can't manage your finances. But of course, I didn't let that stop me, and I complained a lot.

If it wasn't already apparent, I'm a terrible backpacker, maybe the worst, and compared with what I would deem a 'professional traveller', I'm a fucking disaster. I like *luxury*, and backpacking is not luxurious. A lot of the time, it's not even hygienic. Professional travellers concentrate solely on the bigger picture, not the small details. They pay no mind to the person in a shared dormitory who sits on the edge of their bed trimming their toenails, sending nail particles flying all over the floor where they will lie in wait until a sock passes by that they can cling to. Their focus is on thrift – how much money they are saving by staying in a dormitory and the additional travel it will afford – whereas my focus is self-pity, and whether there's enough money left on my credit card to get a private room, or worst case scenario, a six-pack of beer to drown my sorrows. Serious travellers possess discipline, pack their bag in a logical order so they don't have to upend everything to get to their clean underwear, and they are prepared to dry themselves after a shower with a damp, wrung-out chamois stored in a plastic tube because a towel takes up too much space. They're willing to tolerate public toenail trimmers, farters, snorers and all manner of inconveniences in order to travel longer or farther afield. Dedicated and conscientious, they make budgets and stick to them, eat things out of tins, barter with intent, travel light and, moreover, they travel *smart*.

I hale from the opposite end of the travel spectrum – I travel dumb. I shop compulsively and while the committed travellers are eating sandwiches for breakfast, lunch and dinner to conserve funds, I'm dining at the restaurant across the road and wearing a new pair of shoes. I might *look* the part when I'm carrying a backpack, but I'm really just a broke-ass snob who can't afford to stay in the places I feel I deserve. Whenever I'm flying somewhere, sitting in the sluggish bowels of economy class, I'm always bitter that I'm not at the pointy end of the plane, stretched out in my sky bed and resting my entitled head on a proper pillow, like a dirt-poor Mariah Carey, with none of her singing ability but with lashings of her diva attitude.

I didn't care for the women's prison interior design vibe of Jazz on the Park, but I was happy to have somewhere to sleep that was warm and dry while it was snowing outside, and I really liked the diner down the street. Their blueberry pancakes and coffee breakfast deal was a steal at $4.99, plus tax and tip, and I figured that the blueberries, at least, had some nutritional merit. The stack of pancakes sat like a rock in my stomach for the rest of the day, quelling any further hunger pangs, and the coffee was unlimited, so my appetite pretty much disappeared until the next morning when I did it all over again. It was economical, but a diet of pancakes, syrup and coffee may have been the final insult to an already precarious mental equilibrium. 'Holiday eating' is fine for two weeks, but after three months of it, the wheels start to fall off.

My favourite part of travelling, and life in general, has always been the eating part, closely followed by the drinking and sleeping parts. When you're enjoying Thai food in Thailand, or pastries in France, it's great to eat like the locals, but not so much when you're being served chunks of whale meat in Norway or foal in Iceland. Wanting to try every gastronomic treat native to a particular region in a finite amount of time doesn't necessarily result in a balanced diet – sometimes it can result in cheesecake for breakfast and a hot dog for lunch. And as I discovered in New York City, an unbalanced diet can result in an unbalanced mind, or at least help to knock something that's already wobbly on to its side.

A perverse constant in my life has always been the unreliability of my mental health, and it has proven a fickle travel companion over the years, although I am equally capable of cracking up at home, as I demonstrated from the age of fifteen to twenty-one. My brain really outdid itself, though, on my third day in New York, when I woke up feeling so anxious that I thought I would have to invent a new word to describe it, like *gargantuanxiety* or *anxietosaurus rex*.

If one *must* have a prolonged anxiety attack far from home, then frantic, insomniac New York City provides the perfect backdrop. I'd had mild bouts of anxiety before, which had always resolved upon removal of the source, like at the end of the sleeper bus trip in Vietnam or when the caffeine jitters wore off, but this was different. It felt like a bomb had gone off in my skull, so I turned to Google for guidance.

If you research anxiety on the Internet, you may find, as I did, that one of the listed symptoms is '*afraid of everything*', which was exactly how I felt. When I was depressed I wanted to sleep all the time and although it didn't fix the problem, I was able to escape from my thoughts for a while. Anxiety, on the other hand, made sure I was present for all of the unpleasantness. There was no intermission, no bathroom break – it didn't stop. So I wasn't just afraid of *everything*, I was also afraid of everything *all the time*.

I've always been a worrier, dwelling on things from the past, or fretting about things that might happen in the future with those pointless, negative thoughts running on a continuous loop. To stop worrying, you're supposed to draw your energy away from the futile dimensions of past and future and concentrate on the present. I'd heard that yoga (a practice I was yet to try) teaches you to focus on your breathing in order to ground yourself in the moment.

But caught up in my anxiety, I felt like I *was* living in the moment – a fucking horrible one that went on and on.

I'd felt a simmering undercurrent of worry in the weeks before arriving in New York, mostly as I watched my money disappear and started thinking about going back to work, but afterwards I couldn't pinpoint any particular incident that set me off; I just felt like one giant frayed nerve. My skin prickled all over, my chest was tight and I was terrified of nothing and everything at once. The fight-or-flight response was in full activation without an actual threat presenting itself. The sky wasn't falling, I wasn't being chased down the street or held up at gunpoint, but my brain didn't give a shit about the facts. It was on five-alarm red alert.

The anxiety had escalated abruptly and I hoped that it would leave the same way if I acted sensibly, by avoiding caffeine and alcohol and only eating things that were fresh, green, leafy or made of quinoa. So I did all of those things, but to no avail in the short term. My brain was like one of the cars parked outside in the street that was stuck in the snow. It didn't matter how hard you accelerated, the tyres wouldn't grip the ice and the wheels just turned uselessly, going a hundred miles an hour and nowhere at the same time.

Stress is an unavoidable part of life, and it can be friend or foe. As a person naturally inclined towards laziness, stress has at times served quite a useful purpose in my life. It has got me off the couch, for a start, and propelled me into necessary action. I would never have written a book without it, because what I lack in self-discipline, I make up for in ... no other way. I need a *little* stress to light a fire underneath me or I would be one of those people you see on the news who becomes fused to their furniture because they sat in the same spot for so long. And while stress *can* be beneficial, too much of it can be paralysing, binding you in a state of immobilisation that is devoid of comfort. It's like being under a spell where you stress about how much stress you're feeling and only become more entrenched in your inertia. In the absence of a circuit breaker, stress can progress to full-blown anxiety, which is like a socially awkward stress that doesn't get the hint when the party is over, or the crisis has passed, and moves in with you indefinitely. Anxiety's a real dick.

I was all too familiar with the nuts and bolts of depression before New York, but this level of anxiety was a different beast. It made me wonder if my brain could melt from transmitting distress 24/7 and if so, how long it might take for that to happen.

One of the well-known tools for managing stress and anxiety is exercise, so with no interruption to my agitation, despite my newly installed super-healthy diet, I attempted to 'walk it off'. If it wasn't for the dog shit, and all the snow, slush and ice in winter, there's probably no better place for walking than Manhattan. Built on a grid, you can walk along the same street for what feels like forever, and the numbered blocks mean that you have to put in some effort to get lost. The weather was still rotten, but I started on 106th Street and decided to walk until I felt better.

I walked around 230 blocks (about twenty kilometres) in total, down to the South Street Sea Port and back, and the only difference I noticed afterwards was that my legs felt like jelly and my nose was so red from the cold that I could have led Santa's sleigh out of a black hole. The rest of me remained hyper-vigilant, as taut as the string on a bow. Exercise and healthy eating would never be a bad idea, but in this case it was too little too late, like throwing a glass of water at an inferno.

When Renee asked me what was wrong, because something obviously was, I told her that I was feeling anxious but couldn't explain why, and neither one of us really knew what to say after that. With another two days of walking under my belt, I was burnt out, exhausted and not finding any relief in sleep when I was able to get any. It always felt like I had just shut my eyes for a minute, and when they were open, I was instantly back on the same fearful, monotonous loop. The anxiety wasn't going anywhere, it seemed, and since *it* refused to leave, I decided that *I* would. I thought that if I could get home I would be okay again, that home was somewhere I would feel safe. Leaving New York would mean I could finally step off this unceasing, shitty carousel.

I always buy the cheapest tickets when I travel, out of financial necessity. The only real disadvantage is that you can't change your departure time without a very expensive upgrade (it's usually cheaper to buy a whole new ticket). So while I may be able to afford to leave Australia, there isn't much of a margin for error when I'm away, or if I become unwell unexpectedly. My return flight to Australia was a month away, and departed from an airport on the other side of the United States, but at the rate I was going I would have had a heart attack or ended up in hospital by then, so I did what all proudly independent thirty-something adults do when they're in a fix – I called my parents and asked them to bail me out.

Renee had been sightseeing solo, visiting all the famous tourist landmarks I'd seen on my first trip to New York, and while it was nice to have some time to ourselves, we hadn't planned on the separation being permanent. But then again, I hadn't planned on becoming mentally ill. Since I was already on antidepressants, it had taken me by surprise, although I would have preferred a surprise like finding fifty dollars on the street, instead of, '*Surprise! You broke your brain!*' Telling Renee I couldn't go on to the west coast would have been much easier if I had broken a bone, because a plaster cast shouts that you're no longer fit to travel, while anxiety only whispers, on the outside at least. On the inside, it roars like the ocean.

The next available flight to Brisbane was almost a week away, during which time Renee headed to Los Angeles without me. Even though my ticket out of New York was paid for and all I had to do was hold it together for five days until I went to the airport, I still couldn't relax or calm down. A massive logistical problem had been solved, but my anxiety didn't see it that way. I spent the remaining time hiding in movie theatres, watching any film that was showing to escape my thoughts.

I stayed awake the night before my flight home, listening to other people snoring and staring wide-eyed at the wooden slats of the bunk bed above me, because I was petrified that I would sleep through my alarm and miss my flight. All my hopes and dreams were pinned on the idea that leaving New York would be my salvation.

I took the subway while it was still dark, and arrived at John F. Kennedy International Airport before check-in was open. I was the first in line when it did, then I went straight through the security screening checkpoint and sat outside my departure gate for two hours, nervously waiting to be called for boarding. Until I was actually in the air, I wasn't taking any chances – using the bathroom or going to buy a bottle of water were out. My fear had blossomed into paranoia.

When the plane took off and I could finally look down on the city from the safety of my window seat, I felt some mild relief and didn't care if I never saw New York ever again. It was tainted now. I closed my eyes and waited for my anxiety to subside, but I was still waiting when we stopped to refuel in Abu Dhabi, and in Singapore, and when we landed in Brisbane. I hate that moment when I realise, again, that the problem is me and not where I am, even though the problem is *always* me. Even after a hug from my parents, I was the same wreck in Australia that I had been in New York and would have been anywhere, because as long as my head remained a part of me, the anxiety would, too. That being said, I didn't really want to have it removed, just the part that was going haywire and making me feel crazy.

I made an appointment with my doctor as soon as I got home, and when I saw her a week later I was caffeine-free, eating well and exercising daily, but I still felt like I was going to jitterbug out of my skin. She gave me a book about panic attacks, increased my Zoloft dose and explained that, as well as depression, my medication could also be useful in treating anxiety. Anxiety and depression might have very different personalities, but they hang out in the same neighbourhood of the brain, and often go hand in hand, skipping down the road together and *ruining everything.*

Fortunately, the doctor was right and in a few weeks, I no longer felt like I'd had a carton of Red Bull for breakfast, just tea and toast. It was such a relief.

Pre-New York, the anxiety I was most familiar with was the milder type that came before an exam or a job interview, or after drinking too much coffee – the kind that was expected, a little uncomfortable, but passed like a cloud. Post-New York, I knew better, or at least I knew worse, and while there's never a *good* time to feel like you're losing your mind, my experience turned out to be quite informative when I began working with highly anxious patients in a new workplace. My empathy was sky-high.

Anxiety aside, I couldn't bear the thought of returning to my job in oncology, so I resigned when I found a new job as a nurse in a drug and alcohol detox unit. I would be looking after patients who had issues with alcohol, illicit substances and the police, and often an underlying mental illness. I had more in common with them than I wanted to. In addition to using alcohol as a temporary mood booster, there was another trait I shared with my new charges – impatience. My anxiety had developed over a substantial period of time, yet I expected it to resolve the moment I took a walk and started inhaling salad. Most of the patients in detox had the same unreasonable expectations when they stopped drinking or taking drugs, habits that had developed over many years or even a lifetime, and when they didn't feel better instantly, they felt short-changed. Their lives were as dysfunctional and troubled as you'd expect after years of neglect, and the problems they'd been avoiding were still there, but now they were seeing them all without anaesthesia. For patients who already had issues with depression, anxiety, or post-traumatic stress, getting clean and sober reminded them of the reasons they'd started using or drinking in the first place, and why they'd continued to do so when it was so costly in every way.

Recovery takes time, and if you're used to immediate gratification, having to wait for anything is a big ask. Burying unpleasant feelings with drugs and alcohol is much faster, even if it is unsustainable, like building a fire out of paper to keep warm. You get a flame, briefly, and a welcome, short-lived glow, but then you are in the cold darkness again.

10   Ling Ling Is Dead

I was a little gun-shy about travelling again after my New York fiasco and its unpleasant, anticlimactic finale, but after six months of working in detox, I was not only ready to go but also open to the idea of never coming back. Detox patients were a handful, to put it mildly, and while there was a certain novelty to begin with, being threatened, sworn at and hit up for Valium day and night got old fast. The work wasn't as emotionally draining as caring for dying patients, but it was still exhausting – a lot like looking after badly behaved children, even if those 'children' were middle-aged, because there's nothing quite like abusing drugs and alcohol to arrest your development.

Taking a holiday every six months seemed like the most sensible way to manage the wear and tear of nursing shiftwork, rather than saving up all my leave and taking it in one fell swoop as I'd done previously. By the time I'd worked long enough to store up a sizeable break, I *needed* a sizeable break and there were only so many times nasty, sociopathic patients could tell me to fuck off before I did just that. This time I was fucking off to Borneo and Malaysia, places that were a little closer to home than Paris or New York, although nothing is really that close when you live in Australia, except New Zealand.

My boyfriend, Dave, and I had recently watched *Planet Earth*, an eleven-part BBC documentary narrated by David Attenborough, which shows all the incredible things on earth that humans haven't yet destroyed but will no doubt get around to destroying eventually. One episode featured a bat cave in Borneo (not to be confused with Batman's headquarters) that is home to millions of bats. At dusk, they emerge en masse, forming huge swirling ribbons in the sky as they fly off in search of food. My boyfriend was particularly taken with the spectacle, and suggested that we go to Borneo to see the bat migration for ourselves. I said okay, because it did look pretty amazing, even though I don't 'do' nature as a rule. There were lots of bats where we lived in Brisbane, but they were usually hanging around in the trees outside our window feasting on fermented fruit, fighting loudly and acting like obnoxious white trash. If I wanted to see that kind of activity, I'd get together with my friends and drink wine.

Getting to the cave, which was located in Gunung Mulu National Park (*Where?* My point exactly), involved a series of flights, each in a progressively smaller plane, followed by a ride in the back of a truck to get to our hotel in the middle of the rainforest. Because of the isolation and the restrictions in place to protect the environment, accommodation options in the area were understandably limited – to one hotel, whose glory days were well and truly behind it.

The hotel obviously had aspirations of being a grand establishment at some stage, perhaps in the early 1980s, but now looked dated in a sad way rather than a kitsch way. Besides the pastel décor, there was something heartbreaking about the hotel that I couldn't pinpoint at first, but it became clearer when we had dinner at the restaurant that night. We were waited on, literally, by staff who hovered at our elbows and endeavoured to provide a first-class dining service, which they seemed to equate with stacking the table with as much crockery, cutlery and glassware as possible, and replacing our cloth napkins as soon as we used them. They were trying so hard to please that it made my heart hurt, and on top of that, the hotel was practically empty. Perhaps it was just a particularly quiet time of year, but there were six guests in the enormous restaurant in total, including us, and we were completely outnumbered by hotel employees dressed in elaborate traditional costumes, brandishing spears and shields, who performed a culturally informative show for our entertainment while we ate. They put in so much effort for so few, and received such a pitiful smattering of applause that it made me want to cry. It was like watching a faded star reduced to performing for a handful of people in a shopping centre, and being close enough to see the disappointment in their eyes.

We were staying at the Heartbreak Hotel for two nights, and since we had arrived too late in the day to see the bats' migration on the first night, we left the hotel bright and early the next morning, in the company of a guide and a very small tour group. It was a three-kilometre walk to the bat cave, which was near other caves popular with divers, geologists and people who did not share my claustrophobic tendencies.

The bat cave had a huge entrance, so the idea of going inside it didn't faze me because I would still be able to see daylight, and therefore a way out, but I broke out in a cold sweat when the guide told us about 'cave diving' – scuba diving in underground rivers. Apparently, the water in the caves was so clear that inexperienced divers couldn't tell which direction was up or down and often swam to the 'surface', only to find that it was the bottom. They then became disoriented, eventually ran out of oxygen and *died*. It sounded like a wonderful pastime for suicidal people, and the epitome of eternal damnation for claustrophobics.

The trek through the rainforest, along a winding wooden walkway, was beautiful and surprisingly noisy. Nature seemed to be on steroids in this part of the world because everything looked exaggerated and oversized, and it was loud. A percussion section of insects was accompanied by strange sounds I presumed were birdcalls but could have been whistling monkeys for all I knew. The trees were enormous and some ferns were bigger than cars, but it was the giant snails sharing the walkway with us that were the most shocking. I was used to seeing the small garden-variety snails we had at home, but these ones were the size of bread rolls.

When we arrived at the end of the walkway we discovered that the bat cave actually had the underwhelming name of 'Deer Cave' because it contained salty rocks that deer were allegedly fond of licking, and also perhaps because the title 'Bat Cave' was probably trademarked by DC Comics.

There was one significant advantage to seeing the bat cave on television, as opposed to real life, that I hadn't taken into consideration and that was the blessed absence of smell. Visually, the bat cave was incredible and television could never adequately capture its scale, but in terms of odour, it was hideous. The cave was home to three million bats that produced *mountains* of guano, and the pungent ammonia smell this generated was so caustic it made your eyes stream. If *Planet Earth* had been broadcast in Smell-o-Vision, nobody would ever go there. Like most creatures, bats aren't fussy about where they shit and they'll happily do it where they eat and sleep, but to be fair, I had walked into their sloppy home, and they hadn't come to mine and used it as a toilet. I breathed through my mouth, since my first choice, not breathing, wasn't a viable option. It always makes me feel sick knowing that I'm lining my lungs with minuscule particles of stink, like when I'm travelling on a plane filled with farts.

Swept away by the visual appeal of places I want to visit, the smell frequently takes me by surprise, like the time I went to see the snow monkeys in Japan. Japanese macaques, or snow monkeys, are a bit like pugs – cute and ugly at the same time – but just as I hadn't thought of the olfactory consequences of visiting volcanic Iceland or getting up close and personal with a billion bat droppings, the snow monkeys had surprised me, too. Ostensibly, two of my favourite things, snow and monkeys, were together in the one place, and the photos I'd seen of them hanging out in the natural hot springs, grooming each other and nursing tiny monkey babies, surrounded by snow, were amazing. In reality, there was one drawback, which was that the entire place smelt like boiling monkey shit, because monkeys simmering in a hot spring is kind of like letting a bunch of toddlers loose in a Jacuzzi – none of them are going to get out of the water before they go to the toilet.

After a day of exploring musty caves and seeing stalactites, stalagmites and transparent underground streams, we sat outside in the fresh air, peering up at the limestone cliffs of the bat cave and enjoying a cold drink from a very isolated snack bar as we waited for the evening exodus. It had been sunny earlier in the day, but now it was overcast, and the gathering clouds threatened rain.

'There's a bat!' I said excitedly, imagining that a few stray bats emerging from the cave augured the beginning of the swarm, but their numbers stayed meagre, even though we waited, and waited. The guide and the rest of the group left and headed back to the hotel, and we waited some more.

'It's starting to get dark,' I said.

'Just ten more minutes,' Dave said hopefully, and then it began to rain.

Apparently there were a few nights during the year when the weather was inclement and all three million bats said, '*Screw this, I'm not going out in that. Let's watch* Downton Abbey *and get a pizza.*'

We had ventured out to the cave on one of those nights, our *only* night, our only chance. It was the puffins all over again. My boyfriend was crushed.

Our leisurely walk out to the cave, in the cool, fresh rainforest air was much more dignified than our half-walk, half-sprint back to the hotel in the rain as darkness descended at an alarming rate. Suddenly I felt an enormous '*CRUNCH*' underfoot and screamed. I'd stepped on one of the giant snails and my foot was now inside its huge gooey corpse.

Would I ever learn? Nature clearly wanted me to stay indoors so I could watch documentaries like 'Planet Earth' instead of suffocating on bat-shit fumes and wearing snail-guts for slippers.

The holiday to Borneo and Malaysia was the second-to-last trip that Dave and I took together before we broke up. We shared a lot of similar interests, including a love of music, sleeping and eating our faces off, but we usually didn't want to do the same things when we went on holiday, which is why breaking up, once you're past the really painful part, has a bright side. You can stop saying yes to things you already know you want to say no to, such as snowboarding.

I have never been one for sports, really. I had tennis lessons in primary school, and at the end of the summer, the coaches gathered us all together for an awards presentation. I received the award for 'Most Improved Player' and an Emrik tennis bag because, as the tennis instructor so tactfully put it, 'When I first saw this kid pick up a racquet, I thought it was going to be impossible to teach her anything. She was *hopeless*.'

I've never been good at tennis, but I was apparently less bad at it at one stage, although any nascent ability had lapsed before my first year of high school. Reading a book, drawing or watching a movie was my idea of a good time, not running around on a court in an Australian summer, pouring sweat and acquiring colonies of freckles on all exposed skin. Swimming wasn't really my thing either. I loved being in the water, largely because we lived in a country town that was hotter than the sun for eleven months of the year, but I didn't have any interest in taking it further or joining a swim club. That would require discipline, and anything that demanded discipline from me was going to remain a pipedream.

The idea of snow sports was more appealing because I had no concept of what it would actually be like (cold, wet and treacherous) since I had only ever seen snow on television. I'd grown up in a dry dirt bowl swept by the occasional dust storm, so snow seemed magical and exotic, especially compared with brown dust. I didn't see snow until I went to England, although a classmate in primary school had once brought an ice-cream container of 'snow' for 'show and tell', which he claimed to have collected from a mountaintop but had probably just scraped out of his freezer because it had a weird, frozen-pea smell.

As a child, the closest I came to participating in winter sport was visiting an ice-skating rink in Adelaide. I could stand up and stay up, eventually, but I had big problems stopping and would just slam myself into the side of the rink and grab on to the rail. When I finally tried snowboarding, I found that my lack of braking ability had survived into adulthood, fully intact. Stopping has always been an issue for me. I have an addictive personality, so it's much easier not to start than to try and hold myself back when there's already some momentum. Snowboarding was just like drinking – it seemed a good idea, but once I got going I couldn't stop, and it always ended with me disgracing myself.

I agreed to a two-week snowboarding holiday in Japan with Dave, my brother, Michael, and my then eight-year-old niece mostly because the athletes in the winter Olympics made it look easy. I was confident that I would pick up snowboarding in no time, although I had little reason to believe so given that I was crap at skateboarding, surfing or indeed any activities that required poise and balance, and I possessed zero core strength.

Wearing hired snow gear, which didn't look nearly as cool or flattering as I had hoped it would, we hopped on the courtesy bus that left from our hotel near Nagano and headed to the slopes. It was the first time any of us had been to the snow and kitted out in our puffy waterproof suits, we were chubby-thighed and excited. I couldn't wait to start having a whale of a time.

Snowboarding turned out to be a cinch for the first ten seconds. I just stood there, pushed myself a little and took off. With my feet buckled into my boots and my boots bolted to the board, stopping, however, wasn't so cut and dried. In fact, it was almost impossible. Terrified by my accelerating speed, I ended up diving face-first into the snow, which was painful, especially when my legs continued on down the hill and only wrenched to a sudden, violent stop when my torso refused to follow.

'This is how you break your legs,' I thought. And as Michael catapulted himself down the hill, landing heavily several metres away, I learnt that it was also an excellent way to break your ribs. He broke two, as he discovered after an X-ray back in Australia. However, he has an insanely high pain threshold, so he *continued snowboarding*, a little more cautiously and with his grimace the only indication that something was awry. Fortunately, the only parts of me that were broken were my dreams, spirit and pride – all things I could do without.

I was ready to throw in the towel after the first twenty minutes of falling down and struggling to get back up, so I decided to use my snowboard as a makeshift toboggan, which turned out to be another terrible idea. Flying down the hill at a frightening pace, my board threw up a fine spray of powdered ice that blasted into my face and lungs and made breathing almost as difficult as seeing. I stuck my boots out, jamming them into the snow as I desperately tried to brake, but that just created twice as much blinding ice spray and didn't slow me down at all. There was no way I could stop, so I rolled off and the board shot sideways like an errant rocket, disappearing into a thicket of trees.

As I trudged through waist-deep snow to retrieve the board, I had some time to think, namely about how much I hated everything and that I was really too old to be strapping my feet to an ironing board and throwing myself down an icy slope on it.

'Maybe you should try skiing instead?' Dave kindly suggested when he saw the sour look on my face as I emerged from the trees, covered in snow and an air of defeat. He had taken to snowboarding instantly and could see that I clearly did not share his enthusiasm.

I began to wonder if skiing *would* be better – at least I'd have sticks to hold myself up, but then I saw my snow soul brother. He was wobbling unsteadily while his girlfriend and a skiing instructor both shouted helpful suggestions and words of encouragement at him. In spite of the abundance of good advice, it seemed that the harder he tried, the worse things became. His skis veered dangerously out to each side, and threatened to do the splits before he toppled over into a snow bank. He rolled on to his back, swore and pegged one of his ski poles into the air. He was me on skis, and I was probably him on a snowboard. It was like looking into an uncoordinated mirror.

Skiing appeared to involve the same basic principles as snowboarding – falling down on slippery cold stuff and wanting to cry from frustration – so the prospect of doing either for the next week was about as appealing as drinking a glass of my own urine.

With the occasional break outdoors to have a snowball fight, go for a walk or build a snowman, I spent the majority of the week hanging out at the hotel with my niece, Ciara, who also hated snowboarding. We read books, drank hot chocolate and watched the sumo-wrestling tournament on television instead, giving the sumos new names like 'Sad Man' and 'Mean Guy' as they tried to push each other over. Meanwhile the snow continued to fall outside – everywhere but on us.

When the snowboarding part of our Japanese holiday was over, we went to Tokyo and Osaka for a couple of days, where I made a fool of myself without snow for a change, just to keep things fresh. I have a horrible memory for foreign languages, the swear words seem to be the only ones with any stickability, so I routinely greeted people in Japan with the words for 'thank you' and 'goodbye' and kept saying 'hello' when I meant to thank people. Ciara, who was studying Japanese at school and could ask people where the toilet was and how much things cost in a shop, was mortified. Embarrassing her was the closest I'd ever come to being a parent. Fortunately, my alternative approach to communication – smiling and nodding – translated as polite rather than insipid, and made me look *slightly* less incompetent than I did when I opened my mouth.

My English to Japanese was appalling, but the country's Japanese to English translation wasn't much to brag about either. It could be comically incorrect at times, such as a restaurant menu I saw offering a tantalising dish of 'fish with herpes'. But it could also be brutally accurate. When my brother took Ciara to the Ueno Zoo in Tokyo to see Ling Ling the giant panda, they found the panda enclosure empty with a sign taped to the fence that bluntly stated in English, 'LING LING IS DEAD'. It was either a direct Google translation or Japan's idea of a succinct obituary. For all I knew the newspapers were full of curt statements like 'GRANDMA HAD A STROKE' or 'MY FATHER WAS MURDERED'.

With the exception of deceased giant pandas, there was an abundance of other wildlife in Japan and the Japanese liked to eat most of it. At the Tsukiji Fish Market in Tokyo, it seemed that every possible marine species had been lifted from the seabed and placed on ice. Rows and rows of frozen fish cadavers, some the size of bicycles, were laid out, peering with milky dead eyes, and there was plenty of whale meat on offer, in dark bloody slabs that looked like liver. With ready access to the freshest fish, there were a number of sushi restaurants outside the market with a reputation for serving some of the best sushi and sashimi in the city and my boyfriend was keen to try one in particular.

We waited in line with a lot of Japanese people, and eventually were seated shoulder to shoulder at a long bench, fittingly like sardines, for a ten-course sushi lunch. We had already been to a fugu restaurant and had survived numerous dishes featuring potentially toxic blowfish, so the salmon and tuna belly we were first presented with seemed fairly benign. As the courses progressed, my familiarity with the food diminished. I had no idea what I was eating, but I had agreed to ten pieces of sushi, so I was going to eat ten pieces of sushi and besides, there was nowhere to hide in such a small restaurant. I didn't want to appear impolite and I didn't have a napkin to spit anything into either. My boyfriend, however, relished every dish. He was one of those people who will eat anything: chicken feet, pigs' ears or donkey's dick. I didn't share his adventurous culinary spirit.

The meal reached a traumatic crescendo when the sushi chef hit a small sea creature with a mallet and, as it waved its finger-like tentacles at me, he shouted, 'Quick! Eat! Still alive!'

I was used to seeing sushi moving around, but only on a restaurant conveyor belt – not going through its final death throes on my plate. I wasn't just in a cramped sushi restaurant, I was between a rock and a hard place, with the chef standing in front of me watching my every move. Stifling a strong desire to run crying into the street, I ate it, but I didn't feel good about it. As a reward for finishing the entire ten courses, which I only did so as not to offend the chef, we were presented with an extra sushi plate. Would the carnage *never end*?

'What is it?' I asked nervously, peering at the mysterious white flesh, which, mercifully, was at least still.

'*Eat! Eat!*' the sushi chef urged, and even though I wasn't remotely hungry and felt nauseous knowing that something half-alive was chewed up and sitting in the pit of my stomach, I put the last piece of seafood in my mouth.

It was creamy, salty and tasted quite good. The smiling chef then handed me a menu card with the name of the dish written in English: 'sperm sac of codfish'.

I needed to see a counsellor after that meal.

The food options in Japan were endlessly peculiar and, in addition to the aforementioned blowfish and fish jizz, included such delicacies as fermented squid gut, fried fat, whale, horse and dog sashimi, and crazy kebabs made from every animal part – gizzard, skin, ass – threaded on to a skewer and deep fried or grilled over hot coals. I didn't know that chickens even *had* ovaries, let alone that I could gnaw them off a stick and call it dinner. On the whole, I found it advisable to ask what I had just eaten, rather than what I was about to eat, or better still to avoid asking questions altogether. The Japanese institution, Mister Donut, sold a delicious 'angel cream' donut, and if there were any angels involved in the baking process, I preferred not to know the specific details.

When I'm travelling, I say yes to things that I wouldn't ordinarily agree to, such as snowboarding or eating mystery meat. Removed from my usual environment, it's easier to convince myself that I'm the sort of person I would like to be and not the person I am. I suspect there are two different versions of me, and only one of them is real. The other is a figment of my imagination, the person I want to be when I write my New Year's resolutions despite having spent the previous year, and all the other years of my life, actively *not* being that person. This other, better version of me doesn't eat sugar, has an open mind and agreeable nature and says yes to things like horseriding, yoga, outdoor music festivals and funk bands. But the person who actually turns up, or finds an excuse not to go at all, is a curmudgeon who only says yes to things in order to know what I should say no to in future.

As I get older, I'm starting to let go of the idea of who I want to be and to accept the messy reality of who I am. Thanks for asking, but no, I don't want to climb a mountain with you, and if the view from the top is *really* not to be missed, as you say, then take a photo and post it on Facebook like everybody else. At one stage I would have said yes to ice-skating, but I know that after fifteen minutes of falling down and swearing, I'd be stomping back to the skate-hire place to exchange the world's stupidest footwear for my sneakers, because that's exactly what happened the last time. Now I only go to ice rinks to watch other people fall down while I drink hot chocolate – my favourite winter sport. I'm trying not to give myself such a hard time about it. After all, you can't polish a turd, and why would you try to? Just *flush it* and let it go.

11 Just Say No To India

When my boyfriend of a number of years, Dave, became my ex-boyfriend, my first instinct was to outrun the heartache by fleeing overseas, as if I could leave my feelings behind like I'd attempted to do when I bolted from my anxiety in New York. We had always been great friends so the loss of the relationship hit doubly hard, ending despite all attempts to hold on. My second instinct was to drink, so I combined these interests and went on a two-week holiday with my dear friend whom, for purposes of anonymity, I'll call 'Ricky Rosh'. Ricky and I split our time between Portland, Oregon, and Mexico City, Mexico, and did exactly what *we* wanted to do, so there was no communing with nature, snowboarding or physical exertion, only breakfast mimosas, retail therapy, cake and sleeping late.

We had a great time kicking around Portland, but when we told people that we were going to Mexico City next, their responses were less than encouraging, and mostly consisted of sombre warnings that we might be kidnapped and held for ransom because it was so dangerous. Up to that point I hadn't been too concerned about my personal safety in Mexico because all I could think about was tacos, but the constant reiteration that we *should* be afraid burrowed into my consciousness like a tick and made me a little apprehensive. And I believe that this apprehension is partly to blame for the degree of intoxication we attained the night before our flight to Mexico. It was a poorly timed overindulgence.

Too many drinks before a seven-and-a-half-hour flight is not the smartest thing I've ever done, but sadly nowhere near the stupidest. I stuck my head out of the taxi window like a dog all the way to the airport in case I threw up.

Ricky and I boarded our first flight and, as luck would have it, the plane from Portland to Dallas was completely full, so we were seated at opposite ends of the cabin, stuck in crappy middle-row seats among strangers. I reached for the sick bag in front of me as soon as I sat down, clamped my eyes shut and tried to suppress the wave of nausea breaking over me. The inside of my stomach *really* wanted to be on the outside. I had never thrown up on a plane before, no matter how turbulent the ride, but there was always a first time, and we hadn't even left the tarmac.

'If you're going to use that, can you let me know?' the woman sitting next to me said distastefully, motioning towards the reinforced paper bag sitting on my lap. My mouth watered ominously.

'You'll know,' I replied, and she sighed disgustedly.

I began chanting my silent mantra for the flight, '*Please don't puke, please don't puke, please don't puke …*'

I'm pretty sure the only reason I didn't is because the woman beside me was making the same request to the universe even more ferociously than I was. I fell asleep (a.k.a. passed out) waking with a cracking headache just as we landed with an unceremonious thud on the runway in Dallas.

Ricky and I were hopeful that the next flight, from Dallas to Mexico City, would be empty because there weren't many people waiting with us at the terminal, and in any case, we had seats next to each other this time and god knows misery loves company. In the event that we had to use our sick bags, we weren't going to be copping the stink eye from a stranger sitting next to us, although if one of us cracked, it was going to start a chain of vomiting that would make our row of the plane look like the scene with the pie-eating contest in *Stand By Me*, where the whole place is swimming in barf.

'Maybe we'll get a whole row to ourselves!' I said to Ricky, daring to dream as I sipped on a Sprite. The thought of sleeping horizontally the rest of the way to Mexico gave me the first twinge of excitement I'd felt all day.

We boarded the plane and found that we *did* have a row to ourselves, because the plane was so tiny there were only two seats per row; it looked like 'ze plane' that flew to *Fantasy Island*. The best part was that we were no longer preoccupied with feeling sick now that we were worried we were going to die instead, and that fear was magnified when the turbulence began.

Small planes give me the fear, probably because of a plane crash I remember from my childhood. I grew up in a small country town in South Australia with a population of around 300 people, so when a plane with four local men on board crashed into the side of a mountain in heavy fog, everyone was touched by the fatalities. When the wreckage was found, the men inside were still strapped into their seats and appeared to be sleeping, except for their broken necks ... This was the sort of thing I thought about as we rode a rollercoaster in the sky for the next two and a half hours and waited for the wings to fall off. When our plane finally landed in Mexico City, Ricky and I were shells of the shells of humans we had been in the first place.

If any potential kidnappers were lying in wait for us at the airport, they probably took one look at our shattered expressions and decided to find other, healthier specimens who would fetch a better price. When the driver from our guesthouse approached, he smiled dryly and said, 'Rough flight, huh?'

We could only nod, numbly.

On first impression, Mexico City looked hectic, dirty and colourful. I liked it immediately, and when we arrived at our accommodation in Condesa, a bohemian tree-lined area of the city with a wealth of impressive Art Deco archi-tecture, the deal was sealed. I was in love. There was a golden Labrador called Abril and our room was beautiful with two huge beds, tasteful artwork and French doors that opened on to a patio garden. The journey to get there had been hideous, but as we sat in the courtyard that evening under trees laced with strands of twinkling lights, it was soon a retreating blur.

I slept like the dead that night. I love to sleep and, in theory, I should have no fear of death, because if dying *is* just like going to sleep and never waking up, then I'm going to love it. One of the many reasons I'm ambivalent about having children, other than not wanting to pass on my depression and the world being a hot mess that's only getting hotter, is that I still sleep like a baby and nothing fixes me like a nap when I'm cranky. Laughter is supposed to be the best medicine, but good luck getting me to laugh at anything if I haven't had enough sleep.

We woke up to a sunny first day in Mexico City, feeling miraculously repaired by sleep, and hit the ground running, taking a taxi across the city to an art market and feasting on long-awaited tacos. The city was deceptive. It may have been dangerous, but it didn't *feel* dangerous, and reading the Wallpaper guide to Mexico City, a tiny travel tome that pointed out new design stores, galleries, bars and restaurants, made it seem even less so. Gastroenteritis, or 'traveller's diarrhoea', is practically a given in some developing countries, and I knew better than to drink the tap-water, sip beverages served with ice or eat anything that wasn't freshly cooked, but the restaurant across the street looked too cool to be a threat plus it was Ricky's birthday. I let my guard down, and as soon as we were seated at a table in the courtyard, I forgot everything I knew to be sensible and true. I ordered a salad, a margarita with ice, and duck, cooked rare. I went rogue.

The next day, Ricky and I woke up feeling fine, but by midafternoon, we were both a little tired and irritable and put it down to the heat, humidity and not drinking as much coffee as we normally did. We planned to take a trip out of the city to visit the Teotihuacan pyramids early the next morning, so we had a light dinner and went to bed.

It was during the night that all hell broke loose.

They say 'timing is everything', but there's never a right time to be stricken with diarrhoea. Working in hospitals has taught me that the human body is capable of producing incredibly vile odours, and while acknowledging their repugnance, you can usually tolerate those you have generated yourself. In this instance, however, I felt a level of self-repulsion that was ordinarily reserved for the very worst offerings of other people. The smell was as offensive as double denim and as appalling as the concept of humility to Kanye West, but any metaphor falls short of capturing its foul essence.

I visited the toilet, urgently, several times in the night, and Ricky did the same. Whatever was wrong with us, it was fortunate that we both had it, because neither one of us could have forgiven the other if we had been forced to endure it alone. It wasn't just unholy; it was *Rosemary's Baby*–style satanic. The only positive in the circumstances was that every diabolical trip to the bathroom purged a little more of the evil from our bodies, although we began to worry that the reserves were never-ending because no matter how often we went, there was always more. It was like the story of *The Magic Pudding*, where even if you ate and ate, the pudding never ran out, except this was the most disgusting pudding in the world.

The pyramids trip was binned as the tag team pooping carried on into the next day, along with abdominal cramping, sweats, chills and extreme lethargy. Sleep, shit, sleep, shit; that night our room smelt so awful that *it woke me up.*

'Oh my god, this room STINKS!' I railed, throwing open the French doors to let in some much-needed fresh air. 'Oh, no. It's *worse* now! How is that even *possible*?'

A miserable voice carried quietly across the darkness, 'I shat my pants.'

We were losing our humanity.

I thought I was well acquainted with misery before Mexico, whether it was grappling with depression or with the painful breakdown of a relationship, but there's something about not being able to stop going to the toilet that drops you off the lowest rung and into a vile new underworld you never even knew existed. I thought long-ingly of my life before the onslaught of diarrhoea, and the freedom I hadn't appreciated until it was essential for me to be within two metres of a bathroom at all times. The horrible hangover of mere days before seemed like a picnic now that I would happily have stuck a cork up my ass if only it would *make it stop.*

Our defiled room, however, was a hit with one resident of the hotel, Abril the dog, who scratched at our door to be let in and would then lie on the floor, happily sniffing the rancid air.

Inevitably, we ran out of toilet paper and, as I was particularly incapacitated at the time, Ricky was forced to make the shameful trip to the hotel lobby for more supplies, inadvertently alerting the manager of our unfortunate 'shituation'.

There were so many things we'd planned to do during our week in Mexico City, but lying in bed with a churning, gurgling gut and a mortal fear of farting while watching a *Keeping up with the Kardashians* marathon wasn't among them. Before long, we had run out of toilet paper for the second time, and it was just too humiliating to ask for more so I dragged myself out of bed and walked very hesitantly to the nearest corner store. Returning with electrolyte-laden beverages, lemonade, Saltines and a jumbo-sized pack of toilet paper I was rudely reacquainted with the abhorrence of our room after a brief intermission outside in the relatively fresh air. Mexico City may be known for its poor air quality, but its smog had nothing on us.

Ricky emerged from the bathroom with a tortured expression and collapsed on her bed. She sniffed.

'Are you crying?' I asked, concerned.

Ricky looked up at me, her eyes shining with frustrated tears. *'I'm just so tired of shitting!'* she blurted out in despair.

'I know,' I said, sighing.

To avoid spending the rest of our holiday in the kompany of the Kardashians, I dragged my sorry ass through the streets of our neighbourhood until I found a *farmacia*, where I performed a mortifying mime for the non–English speaking staff in order to obtain some

Imodium tablets. Ricky and I took the gut-stopping, butt-blocking medication, waited half a day until we thought it was safe to leave our room, and then headed out into the city in a taxi, crossing our fingers and anything else that could be crossed. We were weak, pale and fearful, but we were determined to see Frida Kahlo's house, despite the clear and present danger that we might use our pants as a toilet. Being kidnapped wasn't even on our radar anymore. Besides, who would want us now? We were disgusting.

I'm pleased to report that we visited Frida Kahlo's house *and* the studios that she and Diego Rivera had worked in without bringing (further) shame to our families or ourselves, which was no small achievement. Buoyed by the victory, our next mission was to reconnect with solid food after having subsisted on bottled water, Sprite and a handful of crackers for several days. Eating was risky, but the medication had worked so far. Although we continued to visit the bathroom excessively, and the output still suggested we were rotting internally, we hadn't done so in public without warning.

Across the road from the artists' studios was the grand San Angel Inn, a fancy restaurant that was once a Carmelite monastery, and while any restaurant was wasted on us considering our pitiful state, it won out by proximity. We were too listless to look for a place that would have been more our speed or budget, like a soup kitchen. The San Angel Inn was the equivalent of an expensive, high-heeled shoe, and we were the stubborn dog shit stuck to the sole that had resisted being scraped off on the welcome mat.

We ordered what we hoped would be manageably small plates of food and sipped bottled water. Neither of us had an appetite, my stomach felt curiously full and empty at the same time, but we desperately needed an injection of energy. I looked around at the well-groomed, smartly dressed people sitting at the other tables. We were sweaty, sickly and pallid, and *we* knew what we had been doing for the last couple of days, even if nobody else did, though I'm pretty sure they could smell it.

'Do you think we're the most disgusting customers who have ever been in this restaurant?' I asked Ricky.

'Definitely,' she said.

A boisterous mariachi band walked around the restaurant, stopping by each table to serenade the customers, grating on our already frayed nerves, and when they approached us my last nerve snapped.

'*No!*' I said, making a stop sign with my hand, and they performed a U-turn and moved on. Then the food arrived, on plates the size of platters and I realised too late that the *pollo en mole poblano* I'd ordered was half a chicken smothered in brown sauce that looked uncannily like shit. Was there no escaping the stuff?

Despite sustaining enduring psychic and olfactory injuries, we were sad to leave Mexico City. And while I had been worried about the top half of my body exploding in a shower of vomit on the way to Mexico, it was the bottom half that concerned me on the way back. Nobody wants to be the person vomiting in their seat, but it's certainly more socially acceptable than being the person defecating. Ricky and I dosed up on Imodium at the airport and prayed that our bowels wouldn't betray us in midair, making for an anxious time in transit.

There's a superstition that bad things come in threes, and we had endured the worst for almost a week. The second bad thing came along twenty minutes into the return flight to Dallas when my iPod stopped working for no apparent reason. Without music, there was no protection from the screaming child two rows away, who continued to scream for the duration of the flight. I guess it was a fairly appropriate soundtrack for a fraught journey.

A week after returning to Australia, I was ten pounds lighter and remained 'symptomatic'. It took another trip, this time to a travel doctor for medication, to recover completely. The doctor had requested a stool sample to send off for analysis, and like a performer struck down by stage fright, my good-for-nothing bum suddenly had nothing to say after weeks of not shutting up. Unable to produce the 'goods', I did my best to paint a picture with words and the doctor nodded her head thoughtfully.

'From the symptoms you've described, and that distinct smell, it sounds like you've had concurrent protozoan, viral and bacterial infections,' she said.

'How does that even *happen*?' I asked.

'Well, it probably came from the water,' she replied, 'water that has faeces in it, from animals or humans, but probably both.'

'*Gross.*' Well, that would teach me to stop drinking shit. I had my own theories about what had transpired. Namely, that the salad I had eaten was rinsed in tap-water and wiped dry with somebody's ass.

I allocate a significant amount of time to worrying. Mostly it's about things that don't really matter, like other people's opinions of me or how I look, or sometimes I am concerned by more important issues, like where does all the rubbish go, and isn't it full-up by now? What happens *then*? Whenever I find myself flailing in my own fretful thoughts, talking it out or going for a walk usually helps, but I know that, if necessary, the ultimate perspective is only a glass of Mexican tap-water away. Diarrhoea has a way of putting every trivial grievance and petty complaint in its proper place and reminds me of what is actually important in life – *continence*. And while I am aggrieved at more frequent intervals by depression and anxiety, at least when my brain is unwell it's odourless.

Although I've spared none of the details when discussing the lowlight of our week in Mexico City, I definitely left the country with more than just digestive issues. It had given me time out to lick my wounds and provided a welcome distraction in the aftermath of the break-up. It had also given me a glimpse of Ricky's dirty laundry and, for a change, a tale of woe and poo set *outside* of a hospital to tell all the folks back home.

As a rule of thumb, the worst travel experiences tend to make the best stories, and the best travel experiences are bilge in the story department. Nobody wants to hear your riveting tale about a moderately priced hotel being clean and tidy or how well you slept on the chiropractic mattress, but bring up the skid-marked underwear you found tangled up in your bedsheets, and the world is all ears.

Prior to the purge in Mexico City, I had entertained the idea of travelling to India, but already had some serious misgivings. India was a country that I could afford to visit, but I was afraid to because I had heard so many different horror stories from people who had been there. The question of going to India or not had very little to do with the country itself and everything to do with my desire not to shit myself, where possible, because I expected my gastrointestinal health to fall apart like a wet paper bag the moment the plane entered Indian airspace. Somehow my body would just *know*, cut loose and things would get very ugly.

My friend Rachell had travelled through India after she finished high school, and besides the gruesome stories of sickness, she advised me that I could expect to have no personal space, to be groped by strangers, to see people defecating freely in the streets and to mingle with cows frequently. Admittedly, if India had been a person she could fight, Rachell would have beaten the entire country to a bloody pulp, but for me the only safe way to travel there would be in an astronaut suit.

On the plus side, it sounded as if I wouldn't be lonely in India. On the minus side, huge crowds of people and molestation have never been my *favourite* things, but if tit-grab came to shove, I could live with them. Where I drew the line, however, was diarrhoea. I worked in a hospital and if I wasn't contracting norovirus from infectious patients, I was cleaning up 'Code Browns' or describing the consistencies of bowel motions in chart entries; there was more than enough shit in my life without going to India.

The rational part of my brain recognises that if diarrhoea was all India had to offer then nobody would go there except constipated people and yoga nuts. I also know that India doesn't have a monopoly on disease because I've even fallen ill in Paris – renowned as the 'the city of romance' and renamed 'the city of salmonella' after my last visit. But it wasn't my rational mind that shat itself half to death in Mexico City. That sort of thing leaves an emotional scar.

Automatically tarring India with the same brush as Mexico may seem unfair and wildly ethnocentric, but I recently ate a packet of curry from an international grocery store that cemented my position. It was a vacuum-sealed vegetable curry made in India, and mostly of salt and monosodium glutamate, I suspect, because I had the thirst of a camel afterwards. I also had diarrhoea. As I sat on the toilet, grimacing and wishing that my sense of smell would leave and never come back, I vowed to remain within the mid-range of the Bristol Stool Chart. So, I'm sorry, India, but that's a no from me.

12   Chicken & Waffles

I can hold a mean grudge when I want to. I still had hard feelings about New York City almost five years after the anxiety apocalypse and even though I knew it really wasn't New York's fault, I didn't plan on returning there anytime soon. Life, however, had other ideas.

'Who invited the accountant?' I asked my friend Seja, nodding in the direction of a guy in a suit and tie standing across the way from us at our friend Alana's wedding. His name was Sean and he might have dressed like an accountant, but he actually worked in television and lived in New York. He was also the 'best man' at the wedding and just before the ceremony got underway, he asked if I would take some photos for him. I agreed, but despite my best efforts I couldn't figure out how to use the stupidly placed zoom on his camera, so many of the photos showed tiny people being married in the distance or close-ups of the chairs in front of me. When I returned the camera, Sean scrolled through the photos, increasingly unimpressed.

'Wow, great job,' he said. 'I'll treasure these photos of the backs of chairs forever.'

Photographic skills and taste in menswear notwithstanding, it turned out that Sean and I had a lot in common, most of all a twisted sense of humour and a love of early Weezer albums, and we stayed in touch after the wedding. When he was back at work in New York, he gave me a long-distance visual tour of NBC – by taking photos of the backs of chairs in each of the studios.

We got to know each other pretty well via text, email and Skype over the next year, although we were leading very different lives on opposite sides of the planet. His workplace was definitely more glamorous than mine – he had less chance of being verbally abused, punched in the face or contracting a blood-borne virus courtesy of a dirty syringe, and good for him.

'Rob Lowe was on the show today,' one text read. 'How is your day going?'

'Transgender borderline patient just drank half a bottle of alcoholic hand wash. Business as usual,' I replied.

When I had accrued three months of long-service leave, the lucrative prize I'd had my eye on for the last seven years, I decided to spend the time in New York hanging out with Sean. That thing I said a few chapters earlier about preferring to regret the things I'd done instead of the things I wished I'd done? This was one of them. There was no way of knowing if I would regret going to New York unless I went, and I figured that if it all went to hell I would have plenty of time to rue the day later. It was how

I had got through the first thirty-seven years of life and I'd always lived to tell the tale. Besides, no matter what happened in New York, I had a return ticket, money in the bank and enough Zoloft to last three months, because I was more frightened that my anxiety might return than I was that Sean would be an axe-murderer or, worse, a tool.

The day before I flew out of Brisbane, I got the flu so I looked hellish by the time I arrived at JFK, which was just how I'd hoped I would look. Sean met me at the airport with a bunch of flowers and a stunned expression, not because I was sick, but because our friendship no longer had the buffer of a twenty-two-hour flight (though I was too ill and jet-lagged to register the gravity of the moment). That morning Sean had been going about his business, unencumbered, but by the evening there was an Australian sitting on his couch, shivering under a blanket and burning through a box of tissues. Two relative strangers were suddenly sharing a very small New York City apartment and it seemed, initially, that digital communication was not nearly as bonding as it had appeared to be.

Sean went to work, as usual, telling me to help myself to whatever was in the fridge or the cupboard and leaving instructions on how to use the television remote control while I rested and recovered from the flu. The only thing I ever feel like eating when I'm sick is Vegemite on toast, so I was happy to see half a bag of bread in the fridge, but then I looked at the use-by date – May 10, 2012. I had arrived in October, and even more worryingly, the bread wasn't mouldy. Whatever it was made of, it didn't seem to be food.

I spent two days in bed feeling like absolute horseshit, and then I was well enough to venture out of the apartment to the Bagel Mill on the corner.

'What kind of bagel do you want?' Sean asked me.

'Um, what are you having?'

'An everything bagel with cream cheese,' he replied.

'Oh, okay, I'll have the same,' I said, wanting to be agreeable but having no idea what I'd just ordered. 'And a coffee with milk.'

An 'everything' bagel wasn't as overwhelming as it sounded, because it's not like a hamburger with everything, as I had feared, but a bagel that's rolled in garlic, onion, salt and seeds that made my tastebuds want to weep with joy. The coffee was another story; it made me want to weep regular tears, the kind traditionally accompanied by feelings of sadness and disappointment. I knew better than to ask for a 'flat white' in America, as I had done on my first trip to New York, only to be served a blank stare in return, and after a while I had started going to Starbucks. I wasn't a fan of their coffee, but at least I knew what I was going to get, and to venture outside familiar parameters was to risk ending up with bitter, burnt swill to drink, which is exactly what I found inside my paper cup.

After a couple of politely restrained, moderately awkward days, I was still blowing my nose and awake at all the wrong times and Sean was still freaking out, but he had devised a strategy for managing this strange, unsettling situation.

'So, I was thinking about this,' he said. 'I'm just going to pretend that you're visiting from New Jersey and that we're dating for a couple of weeks. That way, this will feel more normal and there'll be less pressure.'

I blew up at him, mostly because he had picked *New Jersey*, which insinuated that I enjoyed listening to Bon Jovi, but it felt good to clear the air after tiptoeing around each other. Talking relieved some of the tension we were both feeling, because there was nothing normal about suddenly going from a long-distance friendship to living together. I was beginning to think that coming to New York was a mistake, *again*, and told Sean that I would find my own place in the city, but he asked me not to leave, so I stayed.

Next came the merging of two rather different personalities in a shared space. Sean couldn't cook and I hated to clean, so we complemented each other in that way, but in other ways we were less suited. I couldn't function without coffee and he didn't like hot beverages. He liked scary movies and I hated them. There was no sport he wasn't prepared to watch on television, and none that I would. He is Jewish and I am one of those lapsed Catholics who know they're going to hell but aren't fazed because all their friends are going to be there, too. The one thing we had in common was that we were both used to living on our own, and it showed. At the end of my second week in the apartment, Sean called me into the bathroom.

'Uh, would you mind pulling the shower curtain all the way across after you've had a shower? Like so?' He demonstrated. 'And could you squeeze the toothpaste from the bottom of the tube instead of from the middle?'

I stared at him.

'These are kind of my pet peeves.' He smiled, somewhat apologetically.

'Oh, okay,' I replied. 'Well, do you know what my pet peeves are?'

He paused, sensing danger. 'No; what?'

'Listening to your fucking pet peeves.'

We ended up getting married a year later, and sometimes I crush the toothpaste tube and leave it in a crumpled mess on the side of the sink, just because I know how much he likes it.

For a flighty, commitment-phobic person like me, who never wants to sign a lease on an apartment because it means I'm tied to a certain place for a certain amount of time, getting married turned out to be surprisingly easy. Previously, I would have elected to be hung from a tree and beaten with a stick like a piñata rather than be legally bound to someone for life. And whenever I tell Sean that I want a divorce, like when he puts American football on the television or tells me that my snow globe collection is an eyesore, he just says, 'Don't threaten *me* with a good time.'

He makes me laugh.

I hadn't been applying for nursing jobs overseas or taking steps to emigrate, but I'd always had a feeling that I would end up living somewhere other than Australia, and while *most* of me had been committed to my life in Brisbane, not all of me was. Even though I had great friends, my family nearby, a job I didn't hate (the best possible outcome for me), and nothing to complain about except six months of subtropical heat and humidity, I still felt that a different life was waiting for me elsewhere. It was a feeling that fed my unwillingness to commit, to make ties that couldn't easily be broken, or to put down roots that I would be reluctant to unearth. It's why I didn't get a dog. But if someone had told me what was coming, that I would, technically speaking, be able to say that I was a writer living in New York City, I would have said, 'Drop that bag of glue you're huffing, go outside and get some fresh air into your brain!'

Watching *Sex and the City*, I had aspired to the life of the fictional Carrie Bradshaw, but had glossed over the 'fictional' part of the scenario at my peril. I wanted to live in a spacious New York apartment, write for a living and have an inexplicably luxurious lifestyle and a lot of expensive clothes, despite a seemingly lacklustre work ethic and a parallel income.

Disappointment is an unavoidable part of life, perhaps more so for dreamers, so it's a theme that features heavily in mine. I dream big, and when life doesn't deliver big, the crash landing into reality can be brutal and the disillusionment biting and long-lasting. My dream of being a writer in New York had come true, but I soon realised the magnitude of the fiction I had pinned my hopes to, because other than geographical coordinates, there was little correlation between my life and the romanticised version I had expected as a result of watching too much television.

You couldn't swing a cat in our apartment (pets weren't allowed in the building, for a start), only half the clothes I had would fit in the shared closet space I was assigned, and I don't recall anyone on *Sex and the City* wondering why their apartment building frequently smelt like boiled cabbage, or having to swaddle themselves in a blanket in winter because their radiator had two settings: the heat of Mt Vesuvius and off.

My life in New York was like a Cubist Mr Potato Head, all the features were there, but in the wrong places; it just didn't look the way I thought it would when I got there. I didn't look the part either, perpetrating heinous crimes against fashion behind closed doors, and occasionally outside, too. If anyone but Sean and the Real Housewives of Beverly Hills saw what I wore in the comfort of my own home while writing, they'd be horrified, because the attire itself tells a story, that I don't feel the need to impress anyone anymore and I've given up trying.

Transplanting my entire life to the other side of the world was not as painless as I'd hoped and I felt an unexpectedly deep sense of loss when I left Australia. At first living in Manhattan was a novelty, but it quickly wore off, and even though I was in New York, surrounded by other people and not living somewhere dull and isolated like East Buttfuck, Kentucky, I felt lonely and lost.

As the cogs of the immigration process slowly turned, there was a six-month period where I wasn't allowed to work in the US and even when my work authorisation came through, my Australian nursing credentials weren't worth the paper they were written on, so I had plenty of time to think, which has never done anybody any favours, least of all me. Olympic athletes choke when they think too much about what they're about to do, and I possess nowhere near their mental fortitude. Too much of a good thing, like free time, cake or champagne, can be toxic.

I have always used food to bolster my mood, and manage my boredom, and the one thing that New York City has in spades, besides tourists, rats and opportunities for carb loading, is things that I want to eat. Before I came to America, I didn't know that cake truffles or rice pudding restaurants existed, or that fried chicken and waffles was a 'thing'. I knew about fried chicken and I knew about waffles, but I was unaware that putting them together and dousing them with syrup was something that I could do at breakfast time without being judged. It was a part of my new life that I warmly embraced.

Emotional eating, the kind where you stimulate the unresponsive pleasure centres of your brain with sugar, flour and butter, is particularly appealing when you're in an aimless limbo, and while it means that feeling flat is going to turn into feeling fat, at least you'll be lifted, briefly, until the effect wears off and you're reminded that the emptiness you feel is not actually in your stomach. Cake is not intended to be a substitute for your best friends, it's not even supposed to be a substitute for fruit, but like alcohol, it tricks your brain into thinking it's happy and helps to distract you from your feelings for a little while.

When I had been working as a nurse, the idea of *not* working promised an endless Christmas Day, but in reality, the shine of gainful unemployment wore off after a month or two, perhaps as my memory of employment retreated, and the only cure for work nostalgia is another job. Work was an effective way of escaping my thoughts and getting outside of my own head, and nursing had been a big part of my former day-to-day life and my identity. Of course, when I was at work, all I wanted was to be on holidays forever, and now that I was on holidays forever, or it was beginning to feel that way, I missed the good things about having a job that I hadn't paid much attention to at the time: the social interaction, the sense of purpose, the perspective, and the money. Having a job sucked, but it made holidays even sweeter, just like having diarrhoea reminded you how fantastic it was to *not* have diarrhoea. But that's life, isn't it? You can't see the wood for the trees, but when you can, all you want to do is burn down the forest.

New York City is called 'the city that never sleeps', except in my apartment, where there's a whole lot of sleeping going on. There's a Starbucks on every other block and I don't know anyone, other than Sean, who doesn't drink coffee like it's going out of style, so maybe that's the cause of New York's endemic insomnia. Late-night television talk shows are an American institution, and they *start* at 11.30 p.m., with an even later option following at 12.35 a.m., so it's really no wonder that people are yelling at each other in the street and leaning on their car horns all day. If I stayed up until two in the morning watching television, I'd need a grande dark roast to pry my puffy eyes open and would be as cranky as a bear for the rest of the day, yelling 'Why don't you just *grow up*?' at small children in the park. The entire city needs a bedtime story. They should hand out copies of that children's book for adults *Go the Fuck to Sleep* at the border.

Australia and America are very different countries, despite some alarming similarities such as the genocide of indigenous people, deeply ingrained racism, surging rates of obesity and the advance of cronuts, but one of the most jarring differences I first noticed was on television. The United States Food and Drug Administration allows pharmaceutical companies to peddles their wares to the viewing public, as long as they list all the potential risks of their product in the advertisement.

'*Men, have you grown female breasts since taking Risperdal?*' the television asks, and, '*Does it feel like your antidepressant isn't working as well as it used to? Have you lost your get up and go? Then add Abilify to your regular antidepressant medication!*'

These openers are then followed by a compressed soliloquy of potentially harmful side effects, read by narrators who sound like they've recently snorted amphetamines. For example:

'*SUCH&SUCH-may-result-in-sleep-driving-and-sleep-eating. If-you-experience-thoughts-of-suicide-or-violent-thoughts-or-begin-bleeding-from-every-orifice-please-see-a-health-professional.*'

These ads are supposed to be informative, but they make me tense. Zoloft comes with a small leaflet about potential adverse reactions to the medication, but I haven't read it since 1998, because side effects tend to speak for themselves.

Pharmaceuticals are big business, and in America they really *feel* like a business, with medications being sold in commercial breaks like breakfast cereal or shampoo. In Australia, the closest I had ever come to this sort of merchandising was when drug company representatives would turn up to the hospital with lots of free pens embossed with the name of the drug they were pushing and baked goods to try to win over the staff. In America, it was all out in the open, and if the pill (or pills) you were currently taking didn't work? Throw another one into the mix! The more the merrier!

Sandwiched between the advertisements for antidepressants and blood-glucose testing strips are ads for an egg and sausage waffle sandwich (made with waffles in lieu of bread), thirty different kinds of Doritos and sugary breakfast cereals, as the junk 'food' companies ensure an ongoing market for reparatory pharmaceuticals. There's a medication to treat the high blood pressure and reflux you get from subsisting on donuts, burgers and no exercise, but whatever you do, don't modify your diet in any way or god forbid, go for a walk. It's not profitable for huge corporations, and beyond that, it's un-American.

And if you're unlucky enough to find that you have cancer, the television is also happy to guide you to a fine treatment centre that will have you back teaching Zumba class in no time, unless your health insurance isn't accepted, or you don't have any, in which case, it's been nice knowing you. I'll send flowers.

People are in a hurry in New York City and waiting in line, slow walking and Sunday drivers are not quietly tolerated, so it's a city of services and short cuts. Seamless will deliver the food you ordered online to your door; someone will wash and fold your laundry; someone else will walk your dog and look after your kids if you're too busy, which you probably are because who isn't? Every couple of steps there's a spa where ladies are waiting to cut your toenails and paint them any shade you desire so that you don't have to take the time out of your hectic day to tend to such menial tasks. There's nothing in New York that someone won't do for you if you have the money, so a quick fix, in the form of pharmaceuticals, is another appealing short cut, *and* you don't have to modify your behaviour in the slightest. You can just sit on the couch, watching television, until you feel better.

When I'd almost run out of the Zoloft I'd brought with me from Australia, I was forced to navigate the American health care system – a daunting prospect given that its reputation is about as favourable as Scientology's. However, it was less intimidating than I first thought because upon entering the sacred institution of marriage, I had inherited health insurance. I had options, even if it's impossible to have a relationship with the American health care system that *isn't* complicated. I started by visiting a twenty-four-hour emergency care clinic and was given a list of 'primary care' doctors in my area of the city. I then had to call each clinic to find out which ones accepted my type of health insurance.

My new doctor was friendly, chatty and Jewish, and I know this because after being asked if I'm a smoker (I'm retired) and having my blood pressure and temperature taken, he quizzed me. 'Guess how many Jewish people there are in the world?'

'I don't know. How many?' I asked, thinking this was the beginning of a joke.

'Well, if there's a billion Catholics, and a billion Muslims, how many Jewish?' he persisted. Clearly this wasn't a joke; it was a 'teachable moment'.

'Um, I have no idea,' I replied, which was true.

'Just guess!'

'Okay, uh, I'd say in the millions …' I said cautiously.

'Well, *obviously!* Come on, pick a number!' he prompted me.

'Um, I'll say … a hundred million?'

'THIRTEEN MILLION!' he said triumphantly. 'That's all! Just thirteen million; and they're *still* trying to get rid of us.'

'Really?' I said surprised. 'Well, you sure make a lot of noise for a small group.'

At home in Australia, appointments with my doctor were usually brief and to the point. If I'd ever sat in the room for more than the allotted five to ten minutes just to chew the fat and talk about life or religion, I would have been forcibly removed from the premises. In my doctor's office in New York, though, I had found the one place in the city where nobody was in a rush.

What was supposed to be a routine appointment to get a new script turned out to be a thorough, two-hour medical examination and history lesson, where I learnt that I had a heart murmur, impaired pulmonary functioning and that Jewish symbols could be found on the American dollar-bill. It seemed he'd been waiting for a new immigrant like me to come along so he could finesse his well-considered views. Even when the phone rang, which it did, twice, he would answer it, and say, 'I'm busy right now, tell them I'll call them back,' then hang up and resume talking.

I begged the universe to make him stop because I hadn't had breakfast, my hunger was building and there seemed to be no end in sight. Yes, I knew more about the benefits of gun ownership than I had when I woke up that morning, but what I really needed was food. When he made the point, 'and if Syria goes nuclear then that's it – the world is *over*', I stopped biting my tongue.

'This conversation really isn't helping my depression,' I said.

'Oh, right,' he said with a laugh, returning to the business at hand.

It took twenty seconds, right at the end, for him to sort out the script. I'd never had to work for my medication before, but this really felt like work. It was exhausting.

'So, we still friends?' the doctor asked, smiling.

'Sure,' I replied. 'Now I'm going to go out and buy myself a gun. You've convinced me.' I was being sarcastic, but the thought did occur to me that bringing a gun to my next appointment might encourage him to get to the point sooner.

'Don't knock it until you've tried it!' he said. 'Shooting ranges are a *lot* of fun.'

As I was about to leave, he gave me a hug and said cheerfully, 'Welcome to America!'

And on my birthday, he sent me an email wishing me many happy returns. It was a new frontier in medical 'care'.

When my blood results were emailed to me a week later, I discovered that the only significant anomaly was that I was deficient in vitamin D, possibly as a result of seeing plenty of snow over the winter but rarely a sunny day, and having spent an inordinate amount of time indoors writing. It has been suggested that vitamin D may play a role in depression, and that a deficiency could exacerbate depressive symptoms, but it's a theory that's hotly contested, just like many others: *Fat is bad for you! No, wait, fat is good for you!* 'Studies show' that science can't make up it's fucking mind about anything.

Living in Brisbane for twelve years, a city with two seasons, really hot and less hot, I had never been short of sunshine and I took for granted its beneficial effect on my mood, although I didn't miss its effect on my skin. New York City is a place where anything you could possibly want is at your fingertips, but regular exposure to sunshine from October until April is not one of them. And if the sun is shining outside, it might *look* warm, but without a protective cloud cover, the temperature plummets and encourages hibernation.

The price you pay for living somewhere with clearly demarcated seasons can also be seasonal affective disorder, although the symptoms – low mood, poor concentration, a tendency to oversleep and overeat, social withdrawal and crying spells – also accurately describe what happens when you move to the other side of the world, leaving behind your loved ones and everything that is comfortable and familiar. So there was really no way of knowing if I was sad in New York City or just had SAD. Either way, I was looking forward to summer and the smell of garbage boiling in the sun.

'Ladies and gentlemen, I'm sorry to interrupt, but I'm homeless and hungry, and if you could spare any change or any food, sandwiches, cookies, anything at all, I'd really appreciate it. God bless.'

It was common to see people panhandling for food on the subway, and since Sean and I were on our way to a 'brunch', we happened to be carrying a container of freshly baked pear and ginger muffins, still warm from the oven. We had food to spare, so we spared it.

'Here you go,' Sean said, handing the man a muffin from the container.

'Next time, not with your hands, please,' the man admonished him before sticking the muffin in his mouth.

Beggars *could* be choosers. The sky was the limit. This was *America*.

I used to feel like I was on the world's longest holiday in New York and that before long I would be getting back to my real life, to my job as a nurse and my family and friends in Australia, but when my green card denoting 'Permanent Resident' status arrived in the mail, it sunk in that I wasn't on holiday anymore, I was an *immigrant*. The immigration process, though protracted, hadn't been too difficult because a lawyer had taken care of the reams of tedious paperwork for us, and the final hurdle was an interview to prove that our relationship was genuine, and that I hadn't married Sean just so I could get a job that paid ten dollars an hour and spend an inordinate amount of time trying to avoid stepping in dog shit. Although a lot was riding on the interview, I wasn't that nervous. The worst possible outcome was my being sent back to Australia, where I wouldn't have to pay four dollars for a passionfruit anymore. Poor Sean, however, was a wreck, and his mind kept going blank as he crumbled under the pressure.

The immigration officer asked us questions about where we had met, and when, and quizzed us on other background details such as our families and occupations. When Sean was asked what my job had been in Australia, he struggled to find the right words. 'She was working as a ... nurse (*correct*) in one of those places where they give stuff (*methadone*) to um, people who take crack (*heroin*) ... you know, drug addicts. To make them feel better. I forget what it's called ...'

'Detox?' I suggested.

'Yes! Detox, that's right. Detox.' He blinked and twitched and looked like he was going to pass out.

It's not often in life that you get an opportunity to wipe the slate clean, but that was how it felt when I found out that I had been given permission to stay in the country.

'*Welcome to the United States of America*', the letter began on letterhead featuring the same font as a dollar bill's. '*It is with great pleasure that we welcome you to permanent resident status in the United States.*' I had been given a fresh start, a brand new life, and it was exciting and daunting at the same time.

New York City is a place where people believe that they can be whatever they want to be and initially I thought I might like to be a writer/yoga teacher in my American incarnation. Unlike nursing, with its shiftwork and sleep deprivation, a day job as a yoga teacher would improve my health rather than detract from it; the only issue was that I'd never done more than three consecutive yoga classes, so my posture was horrendous and I had no flexibility whatsoever. But this was my *new life*, and I was starting from scratch, so nothing was out of bounds or beyond the realms of possibility. I joined a yoga studio two blocks away, and *then* I realised that what I actually wanted to be, for a time, was a writer/slob because yoga bored the shit out of me. Whenever the teacher made the class chant 'Ohhhmmm' I was thinking, 'OHHMMMFG, I really need to find another form of exercise'. The idea of being a yoga teacher was as fanciful as the idea of being a ballerina, except I was aware of my dancing ability and that I was as coordinated as a newborn giraffe.

When you're looking for a job in New York City, and you're a new resident with professional credentials that are as useful as a broken arm, all roads lead to one destination – Craigslist. I approached the listings with an open mind, but ideally I wanted work that paid well, did not involve heavy lifting, physical exertion or body fluids and didn't fall under the umbrella of prostitution or crime. Craigslist was something I'd previously only associated with *Law and Order SVU* and serial killers, but apparently it had more to offer than sexual assault and murder. Craigslist was actually a condensed suburb of possibility contained in the original land of opportunity. There was an array of eye-catching headings that screamed out at me, although not necessarily *to* me:

Bipolar and Currently Depressed? Volunteers needed!

Seeking Self Harmers (NYC, all boroughs)

Pretty Girls With Pretty Feet Wanted! $500–$600 Per Night!

(I'm not making this up.)

DO YOU LOVE ANIMALS? ☺

I *did* love animals, so this position sounded like it would be more my cup of tea than indulging a foot fetishist. When I was working at the hospital, and especially when I was being yelled at by a patient or cleaning up diarrhoea, I often asked myself why I hadn't pursued a career working with animals instead of people, as a veterinary nurse instead of a human nurse, and I could never come up with a good answer, but then I read the details of the position and came up with an answer as to why I should not be a dog-walker, either. The pay was atrocious.

If I could give a minimum commitment of nine months, and assuming that the *three weeks* of training went well, I could have a job walking dogs in all of New York's various weather conditions, rain, hail, snow and hot as a wood-fired oven, for the princely sum of eight dollars per dog. I would be required to supply a resume, because god only knows you need one to put one foot in front of the other while holding an animal on a lead, and, in addition to proven leash mastery, some writing ability would also be beneficial in the position. Part of the job would include completing a diary of the dog's 'activities'. That was a nice way of saying that you needed to let the owners know if Fido had taken a dump while he was out pounding the streets with you, as expected, so they didn't have to schedule an evening turd clean-up service, or if anything remarkable had happened, like the dog eating a dead pigeon or a paper cup.

'*DON'T WASTE OUR TIME IF YOU'RE NOT 110% SERIOUS ABOUT OUR BUSINESS!*' another ad warned me in shouty type. Well, all their cards were out on the table, so I felt comfortable reciprocating – I was definitely *not* serious about their business, whatever it may be. An aggressive tone, coupled with a poor grasp of the concept of percentages, didn't sit well with me, so I took this one no further.

'*You will be working seven days a week,*' an 'exciting new start-up company' informed me. I smiled at that. Not in this lifetime, I wouldn't.

I might live in America, but I have an Australian work ethic, or more realistically, about half of any nation's work ethic. I work to live, I don't live to work, and the idea of a seven-day working week is laughable to me, but obviously not to the competitive workaholics who populate New

York. In that regard, I could not be further from where I am meant to be, because I would rather die than wear a pantsuit, and I'll 'take a meeting' when hell freezes over or Anna Wintour gets a new haircut, whichever happens first.

Coffee shops in Manhattan are not so much coffee shops as makeshift offices, with everyone sitting at a table for hours with their laptop open in front of them, talking on the phone or holding a business meeting in person. Over the muzak, the noise of the coffee machine and a couple of grande skinny vanilla lattes, are conversations peppered with phrases like 'reaching out', 'moving forward', 'leverage' and 'lots of moving parts'. And while coffee in North America has a reputation (among Australians, at least) for tasting like ass, it's not used in the same way in New York. Sean doesn't believe in any sort of hot beverage, so he was already out of his element when we went to a café once so I could get a coffee. When I went to sit down at a table in order to drink my scalding liquid like a civilised human being, he had looked at me like I was crazy, having never witnessed such an outrageous act before. In New York, coffee is petrol that's poured down people's throats while they're on the move. It's used as fuel to power through a twelve-hour-plus workday, in pursuit of the American dream, and it could be caffeine, ambition or both contributing to the perception that people in New York are rude.

I've encountered some rude people in my life, and been one myself on occasion, but I don't find people in New York to be rude overall. Abrupt, brutally honest and direct, yes, but not *intentionally* rude, although like beauty, rudeness is in the eye of the beholder, and I may have a higher threshold for it than others as a result of working in drug and alcohol detox and at a methadone clinic where rudeness and verbal abuse were par for the course.

Because everybody in the city is in such a goddamn rush, nobody can afford to be backwards in coming forwards when they've got an issue with something or someone. Time is money, people, and if you're holding somebody up, they will promptly let you know, often by shouting, 'GET OUT OF THE FUCKING WAY!' or 'FUCKING *MOVE*!'

It may not be the most genteel way of speaking, but at least you're under no illusion as to what's being asked of you. You know exactly where you stand, and that it's exactly where somebody else wants you not to.

Similarly, '*Give me a* __' is considered an acceptable way to ask for goods in a shop and causes no offence (in New York) because it's an economy of language that's universally understood, whereas a sentence that begins with, '*Hello. Could I please have a* __' is considered rambling, flowery and besides politely conveying your request, also says, '*I am not from here.*'

Besides the stereotype of the rude New Yorker, there is also the stereotype of the neurotic New Yorker widely perceived to have emerged from the work of Woody Allen and later comedy writers like Jerry Seinfeld and Larry David. 'Neurotic' is a term that has declined in use, and has been broken down, like a side of beef, into more specific 'cuts', with labels like anxiety, social anxiety, obsessive-compulsive disorder, or just Jewish. People thus inclined, and who can afford to see a psychiatrist or 'analyst' in New York, probably do, and the people who can't afford or have no interest in therapy, yell about their problems on their phones, in the street or on the subway.

The honesty, and close physical proximity of people to each other in the confinement of Manhattan, segues into an unintentional openness whereby you learn an uncomfortable amount about the emotional lives of the people around you – someone is finding Xanax helpful for their anxiety, someone else is leaving their husband because the bum is having an affair. Talking is free therapy in an expensive city.

The approach I take in regards to my own emotional issues is along the lines of 'speaking when spoken to' because having a mental illness is one thing, but disclosing that you have one to other people is another. I often think that telling people I had cancer, or even leprosy, would be easier because there is an existing currency for physical ill health which means you can speak about it without frightening your friends or co-workers. And while I don't go out of my way to tell people that I have a longstanding mental illness (mostly because I've lived with it for more than twenty years and it's boring), I don't go out of my way *not* to talk about it because it's also nothing to be ashamed of.

Not so long ago, and certainly in my early adult life, getting someone to talk openly about their mental wellbeing would have been harder than getting blood from a stone – the stigma attached to mental illness was (and still is) comical in its absurdity. It's perfectly acceptable to break your arm or have cancer, but don't even *think* about experiencing an illness above the neck, specifically in the large organ between your ears, because that area is strictly OFF LIMITS and always has been. And as long as you don't *talk* about it, everyone can pretend that it's not happening and there's nothing to worry about – '*Nothing to see here.*'

I suspect my grandmother and my great-grandmother thought that the way they felt was just *them* and that any deterioration in their mental health was merely weakness, or the devil's work, and not an illness like pneumonia that could be treated, but we know better now, even if mentioning that you manage your depression and anxiety with medication still carries more weight than it should. It's easier to slap the 'crazy' label on something that's feared, misunderstood or unfamiliar. It's what we humans do.

Talking about having a mental illness, even one as widespread as depression is known to be, is still a bit like telling someone that you can't stop watching pornography or you have a cocaine habit that you're trying to get on top of before your septum disintegrates. It's not quite there yet in terms of social acceptability, but it's miles ahead of where it has been, and people seem increasingly willing to discuss it, both privately and in public. Things are slowly changing because most of us know someone with mental illness or have experienced it ourselves, and the silence of years gone by has given way to a whisper, which is ever so softly rising to conversational volume. Talking about it helps. Talking always helps.

I live on the Upper East Side of New York, an area that reaches from the East River across to Central Park. It's a neighbourhood that has historically been one of the most affluent. And even in this wealthy borough of Manhattan a homeless woman lives on our street. She sits at the same corner every day, unless it's snowing or raining, reading the newspaper or working on a crossword, with her two huge suitcases by her side. At night she disappears somewhere to sleep, but she's always back in the morning, and at Christmas, she found a tree that someone had thrown away and decorated it with tinsel, bringing the spirit of the festive season to her patch. She's as much a part of our neighbourhood as the church across the road, and the pizza place on the corner.

If you walk past her and keep walking west along our street for the equivalent of five city blocks, you end up at 'The Museum Mile', the part of Fifth Avenue that runs adjacent to Central Park and contains famous museums like The Metropolitan Museum of Art and The Guggenheim. Apartments in that area, with suited doormen and Central Park views, fetch tens of millions of dollars, but down at street level, people with trolleys are going through the rubbish bins outside, collecting plastic bottles to cash in to recycling plants. There are worlds within worlds in New York City, rich and poor nestled side by side.

It's still surreal to be here, writing, even if it happened completely by accident and the pay is terrible and whenever I have a headache, I worry that it's Weil's disease, a very New York, flu-like illness transmitted by rat urine. New York City is a place where dreamers bring their dreams, even if those dreams crash and burn and you end up delivering Chinese food on a bike in a blizzard for two dollars an hour plus tips.

Maybe I belong here.

Acknowledgments

HUGE THANKS to the best publisher ever, Alexandra Payne, for her support, encouragement and advice. Like my first book, this one is also entirely her fault.

To everyone at University of Queensland Press, thank you for giving me the opportunity to write another book, and thank you to my editor, Miriam Cannell, who made it much better. Thanks also to Meredene Hill and Bettina Richter, first class book pimps and lovely people.

I'd like to give a shout out to my travel pals for taking such liberties with their privacy and stories, namely Rachell, Rachael, Shaun, Vicky, Darren, Renee, Eileen, Jo, Tony, Greg and Dave. Thanks for all of the amazing, hilarious, horrible times.

Much love to my family and friends, and to Sean, who supported me in every way as I spent months writing, being anti-social and only half-listening to anything he said. You nice guy!

Thanks to my parents, for oh, you know, *everything*.

I'd also like to express my gratitude to everybody who wrote to me after reading *Get Well Soon!* to tell me that my writing didn't suck. When I was struggling with this book, especially, it was lovely and deeply appreciated.

Last, and also least, thanks, brain. Often down, but not out.